Pro
Alberta
1820 F
Calga

Family Matters
Parenting Tips from the Business World

RONI JAY

illustrated by Peaco Todd

Parenting Press, Inc.
SEATTLE | WASHINGTON

GK 600 J38 2002
Jay, Roni
Family Matters
c.1

Text copyright © 2002 by Roni Jay
Cover and interior illustrations copyright © 2002 by Peaco Todd

All rights reserved. No part of this book may be reproduced in any form without permission from Parenting Press, Inc.

Printed in the United States of America
Designed by Magrit Baurecht Design

Library of Congress Cataloging-in-Publication Data

Jay, Roni.
    Family matters : parenting tips from the business world / Roni Jay ; illustrated by Peaco Todd
        p. cm.
    Includes index.
    ISBN 1-884734-74-X   ISBN 1-884734-73-1 (pbk.)
    1. Parenting. 2. Parent and child. 3. Management.
    4. Psychology, Industrial. I. Title.

HQ755.8 J38 2002
649'.1 dc21

                                        2001051370

Parenting Press, Inc.
P.O. Box 75267
Seattle, Washington 98125-0267

http://www.ParentingPress.com
Telephone 800-992-6657 • Fax 206-364-0702

Contents

About leeches and other pertinent matters 5

1. Customer Relations Tips 7

Acknowledge the customer immediately 9
Greet the customer with a smile 10
Consider the customer's viewpoint 11
Find the need behind the request 13
Behave as you would have the customer behave 16
Treat the customer with respect 17
Handle complaints 18

2. Selling Tips 27

Set objectives 28
Prepare alternatives 29
Ask open-ended questions 30
Keep control 31
Sell benefits, not features 33
Handle objections 34
Close the sale 36

3. Negotiating Tips 43

Negotiate a win-win deal 44
Know your bottom line 47
Aim high 49
Look for variables 52
Get all the cards on the table 54
Never give free concessions 57
Agree to all or nothing 58

4. Motivation Tips 61
Show your team the big picture 62
Set clear and realistic targets 63
Inform team members 65
Find the right incentive 66
Recognize employees 76

5. Management Tips 81
Give feedback 82
Handle mistakes 90
Discipline 91
Conduct effective interviews 95
Deal with people who create problems 98

6. Teamwork Tips 107
Encourage mutual support 109
Give each person responsibility 111
Train the team collectively 112
Recognize the team as a whole 112
Avoid areas of friction 113
Discourage division within the team 115
Utilize each team member's strengths 116
Communicate with your team 117
Deal with conflict and rivalry 119

Conclusion 125
Index 127

About leeches and other pertinent matters

Most of us spend several years working before becoming parents, and many of us continue to work once we have children. At work, we learn all sorts of useful skills—managing, selling, negotiating, and so on—which we can apply in any organization we work for. But when we become parents, all those hard-won skills are useless. Or are they?

This book explains how our business skills don't have to be left on the doorstep when we walk in the front door. We may feel that the children get the better of us every time, but here is one advantage we have that they don't: all those business skills we are familiar with and they know nothing about. All we need to do is learn how to apply them to our children as well as to our customers and our staff.

Coping with children can seem like running a department or small organization, which is why the same techniques are useful. Though you can't fire your children or even take a holiday without them tagging along, you can teach them more easily than the adults who work for you. At least, you don't have to contend with behavior patterns that have been set for years.

Obviously, there is no perfect way to handle children so that we don't hear a single whine or tantrum (more's the pity), but there are certainly techniques that make life much easier. These techniques may not always work at three in the morning or when a favorite toy has just disappeared down the garbage disposal, but they certainly work most of the time to make the atmosphere more pleasant. What's more, as we know from our business experience, these techniques work with grown-ups. They are effective with children right through those teenage years, even when, like your customers and staff, they have become wise to the techniques and know what you're up to.

As with any new parenting practices, you'll find that some of these techniques take a little while to establish. Many will go unnoticed by your children—although you'll notice the benefits—but some will be spotted instantly as a change of system.

For example, the very first technique in the book is to acknowledge your children when they ask for your attention. You don't need to drop everything for them on demand, but do let them know you'll deal with them in a moment. They may resist this kind of change for a while (all right, they will resist it until they've tried it), but once they know you're sticking to it consistently, they'll give in to it. After they've given it a fair trial, they'll even realize that it benefits them as well as you. Stick with your new approach, and it won't be long before it pays dividends.

Business skills transfer amazingly well to parenting. You can get real value from customer relations to teamwork skills, as you'll see. What's more, once your kids have finally worked out what you're up to, you'll have done your parental duty and taught them enough skills to set them on a fast-track business career.

All the techniques in this book have a proven track record in the workplace, helping to build more successful and happier organizations. You will find that they have the same effect at home, building more successful and happier families. Follow these guidelines, and you'll soon find that you will be as confident in your skills at home as you are at work.

Now, about leeches: you'll find more than one example in this book with leeches because they were a fixture of my childhood. The medicinal variety of leeches I collected were slimy and revolting, but not poisonous or dangerous. My parents, although more resilient than many, were nevertheless slightly disgusted at my passion for catching leeches from the ditch near our home by sticking my arms in the water and waiting for them to latch on. As far as I was concerned, they were free pets. To feed them, I needed only to stick a finger in the jam jar for a few minutes and then pick them off again. In a similar way, my young son likes to strip off his T-shirt in the summer so that he can stick slugs and snails to his stomach and chest. Having moved on myself, I am now in turn slightly revolted. If you, too, are revolted, feel free to mentally change the example to something that resonates with you and your child.

O N E

Customer Relations Tips

Applying customer relations skills to your children means treating them as you would a customer. You might initially find this whole idea somewhat galling. After all, you're supposed to treat customers with deference and give them whatever they want—hardly a technique that most of us want to apply to our children. And anyway, how can children be like customers when we all know that the customer is always right?

But look at it another way. We treat customers with as much friendliness and cooperation as we can because it works. Sorry to be cynical, but customers like us better and buy from us more often if we treat them well. Sure, the people who really understand customers well do it genuinely and with the best of motives, but there's no denying that it gets the response we want, regardless of our motives. Well, if it works on grown-ups, why shouldn't it work on children, too?

Actually, we know it works on children. If we don't know it, we should. The Disney Corporation knows it. McDonald's knows it. There are plenty of businesses out there who regularly deal with children as customers, and they can vouch for the fact that kids respond in just the same way as adults to the treatment they receive (although the adults usually take it slightly better when they're told that the product they really want to buy won't be in stock until next week).

Here are the core rules of good customer care, all of which will help you get the response you want out of your children.

• *Family Matters*

"Hello! We're busy right now, but your problem is important to us so please wait for the next available parent."

You should be familiar with all of them, so applying them to the kids—once you've got used to the idea—really isn't difficult.

Acknowledge the customer immediately

BUSINESS TIP:

> *Even if you're busy on the phone or with another customer, always let a newly arrived customer know that you've seen her. Find a moment to say, "I'll be with you in a moment," or "Sorry to keep you waiting," or at least make eye contact and give a polite nod to let her know that you'll deal with her as soon as you can.*

Children are even more assertive attention-seekers than customers. A customer likes to feel that he is the most important person to you right now; a child demands to know that he is. Therefore, when your child explodes into the room where you're entertaining friends, or starts asking where his clean T-shirt is while you're trying to change the rear brakes on your car and order a take-out pizza at the same time, try acknowledging him immediately.

Children are a nightmare for interrupting, and every time they do it you're torn between two options, neither of which is appealing. One option is to ignore them, in which case you can guarantee that they'll just get worse (as in louder, more insistent, more threatening, and generally more unpleasant). The alternative is to drop everything for them. This has great short-term appeal—that is to say, it works. But at the back of your mind there's that nagging feeling that you're not being a good parent. You're teaching them to expect people to drop everything for them (obviously).

Acknowledging your children gives you a middle way. You neither ignore them nor drop everything. You teach them that they can have your attention if they will simply wait a moment. What's more, they will get your full attention, instead of the rushed, stressed, "Oh, what is it now?" response that they would get if you dealt with them instantly. When they burst in on you with demands or questions, try saying, "Hi! I'm just putting out this small fire that Amy started, but I'll get you a drink in just a minute." As with a customer, keep the note of (understandable) irritation out of your voice if you humanly can. Using this technique, everyone benefits.

- You get to finish what you're doing first.
- The child may have to wait a moment, but the pay-off is your undivided attention.
- Everyone can stay in a pleasant mood.
- You can give up the guilt, comforted by the thought that you are bringing up your child to be nicer, less selfish, and less egocentric.

Greet the customer with a smile

BUSINESS TIP:

Always get off on the right foot with customers. A smile sets the tone for a friendly and helpful exchange. Even if you can see a customer bearing down on you, looking black, carrying a broken product he bought from you only yesterday under his arm, . . . Smile. It may not solve everything, but it will solve much more than scowling will.

Children are always ready to meet a challenge. The second you raise your voice or sound irritated, they are right there mirroring you in response. To children, the best form of defense is attack. The only effective way to handle this characteristic is to beat them at their own game. Give them something positive to mirror. Let them see that they don't need to employ any form of defense because they're not under threat. If your opening gambit is a welcoming smile, it takes the wind right out of their sails.

If you have any experience with customers, it is no doubt instinctive for you to smile whenever you greet them. Yet when we get home to the kids, this instinct seems to vanish. Of course, there are times when it's natural to greet our children with a great welcoming smile and a hug and a kiss. But how many of us can honestly say that we do it every time we see them?

If you can smile at an angry customer whom you know is about to make a complaint, you can learn to wake with a smile as you say, "Hello, darling, lovely to see you. Gosh, you're not often up at five in the morning, are you?" Simply learn to retain your instinct to greet the customer with a smile, and bring it home with you. See your child as a customer every time you greet her, and she'll soon forget to go on the defensive at all.

Consider the customer's viewpoint

BUSINESS TIP:

> *Never mind that you're due to close the shop in two minutes and a customer wants to launch into a lengthy cross-examination about how exactly the camera he's buying works, and what each of the little buttons on the side do. Look at it from his point of view. He wants to take photographs at the wedding he's going to tomorrow, and he's not good at reading instructions. He clearly needs you to explain the camera to him now.*

You and your customer have totally different agendas. You want to get the place closed and locked up so that you can do the paperwork and then get home and put your feet up. The customer, on the other hand, wants to buy a good camera and then learn how to use it before tomorrow's wedding. You know it's the customer's agenda that counts . . . simply because he's the customer, so you look at it from his viewpoint and you patiently explain (as many times as necessary) how the camera works.

You see it from his viewpoint because you have to. He's the customer, and it's your job to look at things from his perspective. But what about the children? Do you always see things from their point of view? Suppose you are in a rush to get to the grocery store and back home in time to prepare dinner before your guests arrive. Your child, on the other hand, is refusing to get into the car until her favorite television program has finished in twenty minutes. (Mind you, it was never her favorite program before; it just suddenly became her very, very favorite when you told her she was going to have to miss it. If you're magnanimous, you'll overlook that.)

What usually happens in this situation is a blazing quarrel. You get increasingly insistent that she get into the car NOW, she digs her heels in ever further, and before you know it you're not enjoying yourself at all. Nine times out of ten, if you look at it from your child's perspective rather than your own, you'll at least be able to compromise.

Imagine the tables were turned. You've been waiting all week to find out what happens in this episode of your favorite program, and, just as you're getting into it, your child turns up, nagging you to come outside and play. You wouldn't be too pleased, would you?

You'll find that looking at the situation from your child's viewpoint makes it easier for you to cope. Instead of feeling irritated, you feel sympathetic. Of course, she must still get in the car and come shopping, but at least you'll be more tolerant in the way you put it to her. Otherwise, from her perspective, not only are you trying to stop her from watching her favorite program, but you're giving her a hard time as well—insult added to injury.

When you look at the situation from the customer's viewpoint, however, you're more likely to start out by saying, "I'm sorry, sweetheart, but we've got to go shopping." This is altogether a less confrontational attitude. It gives you scope to look for a compromise, too, which you'll feel more inclined to do if you're sympathetic from the start. "How about we tape your show and you can watch it when we get back?" Or, "Why don't we buy some of your favorite ice cream, to make up for missing your favorite program?"

To be honest, the most difficult part of this technique can be working out what your child's viewpoint actually is. The older a child gets, the easier it becomes, broadly speaking, but the depths of a child's mind can be hard to fathom. Nevertheless, if you're two years old, it really is the end of the world if your toy car refuses to fit down that hole.

Once they are old enough to communicate (roughly after the age of two, but before the age of thirteen), you can, of course, ask them to explain their point of view. Simply say, "I don't understand the problem. Can you explain it to me?" Try not to sigh as you speak, but to adopt a tone of genuine interest and concern, just as you do with a customer whose needs happen to conflict with your own.

Once you get used to seeing things from your child's perspective, it gets easier and easier to determine what the problem is, just as it did when you first learned to look at things from the customer's viewpoint. You'll find that you start off with a sympathetic attitude, which keeps the atmosphere pleasant and makes compromise less painful on both sides. What's even more important, your children, like your customers, will feel that they are important to you and that their feelings matter.

Find the need behind the request

BUSINESS TIP:

> Customers often fail to explain fully what they need, which can make it hard for you to help them. You have to find ways to get them to reveal what they really want. If a customer simply says, "I need a hat," it's impossible to know which of your 240 styles of hat she will want. But if you find out why she needs a hat—to keep her hair dry in the rain, wear to a garden party, keep the sun off—you can narrow down the possibilities until you give her what she needs. Do this by probing and asking open-ended questions until you have all the information you need.

Customers have nothing on children when it comes to concealing their intentions. For a start, customers generally keep back information because it hasn't occurred to them that it will help, not because they really don't want you to know it. Children, on the other hand, may have all sorts of deliberate motives for keeping you in the dark. Nevertheless, the techniques that work with customers also work with children when it comes to getting to the bottom of a request.

Older children may well try to keep quiet about their end purpose in case you disapprove. For example, a simple, "Can I stay at home this afternoon instead of coming out with you?" may actually mean, "Can I stay at home this afternoon because

"Can I borrow some matches? It's for educational purposes only."

if you're not going to be here then I can invite all my friends over to watch the unlabeled video Paul found hidden under his parents' bed?" Some judicious probing and questioning here may save you from being lynched by a large group of angry parents who don't like what their children do at your house.

Younger children, on the other hand, assume that you understand what they want when, in fact, you haven't a clue. Often, however, if you can't fulfill their request, you could easily find an alternative if only you understood the problem. For example, when your three-year-old asks you for a sharp knife, it's quite likely that you'll say "no." But if you delve deeper, you may discover that he wants the knife in order to cut himself a slice of bread because he's hungry. Once you've identified this root problem, you can offer to make him a sandwich yourself. If further questioning reveals that he wants to help, give him a blunt knife so he can spread the butter and the filling himself.

The key to finding the need behind the request is to ask open-ended questions. These are questions that require a full answer rather than a simple "yes" or "no" or some other one-word answer. Such questions often start with one of the following words:

- How ("How would having a video recorder in your bedroom be different from sharing the family video recorder downstairs?")
- What ("What are you going to do with the sharp knife if I give it to you?")
- Why ("Why do you want to stay at home this afternoon?")

Just as with customers, you need to ask about the reason for the request, not the request itself. If a customer asks for a hat, don't ask, "What sort of hat?" You'll end up playing "Twenty Questions." If, on the other hand, you ask her why she wants a hat, you can narrow down the choices much faster. If she wants it to keep the rain off, you've narrowed it down to a fraction of your range straight away. Always probe the reason behind the request, not the details of the request itself.

You may still have to ask a series of open-ended questions before you finally get to the bottom of the matter. Concentrate on the hidden agenda and probe it directly. If you ask your twelve-year-old what he's going to do at home all afternoon, he may well simply cover up the truth with, "Oh, just watch a video." But if you probe the reasons—"Why this afternoon, when we're out? Why not come with us and watch it when we get back?"—you make it much harder for him to avoid giving you the information you need.

When it comes to small children, it must be said that there's a certain satisfaction in turning the tables and asking them a series of questions beginning with "Why?" But more than that, it may be the only way you'll ever establish the strange truth of the matter: "Oh, I see. . . . You need a hat to put on your head so you can chase the cat under the table and it won't hurt if you bang your head. Of course, silly me."

Behave as you would have the customer behave
BUSINESS TIP:

This rule of customer care is all about the fact that people respond to us in the same manner in which we communicate with them. If we are always open, friendly, and positive towards customers, our customers will be open and friendly in response. If, on the other hand, we are unfriendly and unhelpful towards our customers, they will be unfriendly and difficult back. This is why some people always seem to attract easy, friendly customers while others complain that they get all the difficult ones. Each of them is generating the response they get.

You have doubtless also observed that some children seem to have negative characteristics that echo their parents' behavior. Perhaps the parents shout at the children frequently, and the children are loud and aggressive in turn. Maybe the parents never listen closely to their children, and then ask, "Why does she never listen to what I'm saying?"

Of course, it's always easier to spot faults in other people than in ourselves. Most of us are guilty of generating negative behavior in our children by behaving negatively towards them. We may not be as aggressive or as downright unpleasant as some parents, but we're not perfect either. More typical, everyday lapses include these:

- Complaining about food in front of the children, and then fussing when they won't eat their greens;
- Interrupting the children when they are speaking, and then telling them not to interrupt when we speak to them;
- Raising our voices as soon as we get angry, and then shouting, "Don't yell!" at the children.

Mind you, what we notice less often is that our children—like our customers—mirror our good behavior, too. The thing is, we are on our best behavior with our customers, but not necessarily with our children. This is understandable; after all, if you were up for two hours in the night cleaning up vomit caused by eating too many sweets, it probably wasn't your customers' fault, so why take it out on them? Your child, on the other hand, is probably not at the top of your list of "people to be nice to" at the moment. Nevertheless, it's in your own interests to treat him well, because he is more likely to respond in kind.

Whenever you notice a characteristic you don't care for in your child, it's always worth asking yourself whether perhaps you exhibit the same characteristic yourself (be honest, now). If you have more than one child, and they all exhibit the same characteristic, the evidence against you starts to look quite strong. If they always start shouting every time there's a disagreement between you, resist the temptation to shout back. Just say, firmly but without raising your voice, "I'm not shouting, and you don't need to either."

Treat the customer with respect

BUSINESS TIP:

Always treat customers with politeness, deference, and respect. This simply means remembering to say "please" and "thank you" to them, apologizing for keeping them waiting, listening carefully to what they are saying, and observing all those little niceties that make them feel they are important to you.

This technique should be child's play with customers. And so it should with children, too. For some reason, we often drop these niceties at home, which is strange; treating people with respect is a way of showing them that they are important. After all, who is more important to us than our children? Perhaps because this behavior seems somehow formal, we tend to abandon it with the people who most deserve it.

This rule of customer care is linked to the previous one: behave as you would have the customer behave. If we don't treat our children with respect, it is rather hypocritical to complain when they show us no respect. Treating them respectfully is the best way to stop them from telling you to "Shut up," or "Give me my clean socks now," or even from simply ignoring you (I'm never sure which is worse).

The point to aim for is one where the family home rings continually to the sound of "please" and "thank you," and phrases such as "Sorry to keep you waiting," "Excuse me," "Would you mind . . . ?" and "Can I give you a hand with that?" All right, perhaps that sounds a little implausible. Actually, it's not so difficult as you think. Just visualize a customer's face superimposed over your child's, and you'll find that it's simply the behavior you use everyday at work.

Handle complaints

BUSINESS TIP:

> *Handling complaints at work means dealing with dissatisfied customers in such a way that you leave them feeling not only satisfied but positively impressed with you and your organization. The kind of complaints you might have to handle range from the minor gripe to the no-holds-barred, claws-out rant. Even the minor complaints, though, would turn into major ones if you handled them badly.*

Naturally, children are much more effective at complaining than customers are. In fact, they make most customers look pathetic. Perhaps the next time a customer says, "Excuse me, sorry to bother you, but this toaster I bought from you yesterday doesn't seem to work, and it's just set fire to my kitchen," the best response would be to say, "Come on! You can do better than that. Wait there, and I'll just go and fetch a small child to show you how it should be done."

Since customers were all children once, I can only suppose that complaining is a skill most of us lose as we get older. Certainly, we tend to make far fewer complaints as customers ourselves than we receive from our children. The good news is that we can handle our children's complaints, whether they are expressed as little whines or delivered at a hundred decibels accompanied by sobs and tears, in just the same way as we handle complaints from customers. It's just a matter of following six key guidelines.

▶ Listen.
▶ Sympathize.
▶ Stay neutral.
▶ Ask questions.
▶ Involve the child in the solution.
▶ Carry out the solution.

▶ Listen

BUSINESS TIP:

The customer is never going to calm down until she has had her say and got her feelings out into the open. Listen until she has finished saying what she wants to. You can help the listening process by asking her relevant questions to show you're interested, but don't make her feel rushed or pressured into shutting up, or she'll become more frustrated.

It's often the case that, where your own child is concerned, you instantly know what the trouble is. But that's not the point, any more than it is with customers. Only half the point of listening is to establish the facts (at least, as the child sees them). The other half is psychological: to allow the child to let off steam, and to feel that you are paying attention to her complaint.

If you don't go through this process, your child (or customer) will carry on shouting: she still feels that she needs to make herself heard. Once she feels confident that you are giving the matter the attention she thinks it deserves (even if you privately disagree), she will have no need to shout. Therefore, the fastest way to calm her down—and prevent your nerves from fraying any further—is to hear her out.

Once you've heard her, let her know you have. Otherwise, she will keep repeating herself until she thinks you've got it. Summarize the problem and repeat it back to her: "You're not happy because it's macaroni-and-cheese for supper and you don't like it. I understand now why you're upset."

▶ Sympathize

BUSINESS TIP:

> Customers are often angry because they are on the defensive: they are worried you'll tell them it was all their fault for not reading the instructions properly, or that you'll look at the toaster and insist that there's nothing wrong with it. The quickest way to reassure them that you're on their side is to sympathize with them. This is not the same thing as apologizing. You can say you're sorry that something happened without saying it was your fault. Or, you can commiserate with how frightening it must have been when the kitchen caught fire.

Children, like customers, are worried that you're going to tell them it's all their fault, or that there's nothing to complain about. They're afraid that you might say, "Well, you ate it last time I gave it to you" (which may well be true), or "Nonsense! Macaroni-and-cheese is good for you. Now just eat it up."

The sooner you can reassure them that you're taking their complaint seriously, the sooner they will move on towards finding a solution and getting the whole thing over with. How about, "Oh, no. So you hate macaroni-and-cheese and this is the second time this week we've had it. You must be fed up to the back teeth."

▶ Stay neutral

BUSINESS TIP:

> Never try to justify your actions—it's really irritating to someone who's complaining. It makes her feel like you're implying that she's exaggerating the scale of the problem. What's more, she is simply not interested in your side of it. All she cares about is that her toaster isn't working. Once you've listened and sympathized, you should find that the customer is calming down nicely. Don't blow it all by saying, "Well, it's not our fault. We don't make these toasters, we only sell them. If there's a problem, it's the manufacturer's fault."

Children are at least as single-minded—not to say self-centered—as grown-ups. Your eight-year-old doesn't care about your side of it, and is extremely unlikely to respond to your defensive comment of, "Well, I can't possibly remember all your likes and dislikes" with a conciliatory, "Fair point. Okay, I'll choke down the macaroni-and-cheese then. No problem."

You may have a perfectly valid defense. Indeed, you may well be in the right. But the odds are that you're better off in the long run getting this outburst over with as quickly as possible, rather than pointlessly mounting a well-argued defense that falls on deaf ears.

There is one other point here. I hate to say this, but it's just possible that your child may be right. It almost never happens, I know, but maybe, just once in a blue moon. . . . What if it is the second time this week you've given her macaroni-and-cheese? And what if your child did tell you on Tuesday that she didn't like it?

There is a simple rule about apologizing: always apologize if it is your fault, and never apologize if it is not. (This applies to customers too, legal requirements allowing.) Assuming your daughter isn't going to sue you for serving up a meal you knew she didn't like, why not apologize?

We frequently demand apologies from our children—for being impudent, for hitting a sibling, for grabbing, and so on. But how often do we set an example ourselves by apologizing

22 • Family Matters

"I don't know what happened—I just asked her to clean up her room and suddenly I'd agreed to redecorate it."

when we're in the wrong? We are often even more defensive than they are. If it's your fault, swallow your pride and say so. Your children will respect you for it (although they'll never admit it).

▶ Ask questions

BUSINESS TIP:

It's time to get on with resolving the complaint. The next stage is to ask questions in order to help identify the options for putting things right. Your questions aim to identify what happened in order to shed light on the problem. Was it the plug or the toaster itself that ignited? Were there any other problems? You're not trying to allocate blame—we've already established you don't want to do that—but you need information. There's no point in sending the toaster off for repairs if a new plug will fix the problem.

Find out as much as you can about your child's problem. Bear in mind that cross-examination can make children feel nervous, so ask in a tone of concerned interest and don't do an impression of the Spanish Inquisition. If serving up macaroni-and-cheese is going to be a problem in the future, you need to find out precisely why before you can suggest a workable alternative. Ask questions such as, "Is it the macaroni or the cheese you don't like?" and "Can you manage to eat it this time if I stop cooking it so often in the future?" and "What do you particularly like?"

Asking questions has the added benefit of demonstrating a genuine concern to resolve the problem. If you're handling this complaint according to the rules so far, you should find that any initial flood of noise and anger has by now slowed to a mere trickle.

▶ Involve the child in the solution

BUSINESS TIP:

> Your customer came to you because she wanted a solution to her problem. Sure, she may also have wanted to let off steam, but in the end she wanted to resolve the problem, so you need to find an answer. It needs to be one your customer feels involved in, can support, and will go along with. This means she has to choose the solution herself. Offer her a choice of options, and let her have the final say. You could, for example, offer to repair the toaster, exchange it for another, or give her a refund.

One technique that works with customers is to ask them, "What would you like us to do to resolve this?" However, you should avoid this if you have one of those occasional customers who is still annoyed enough to be unreasonable and ask for the moon. "I'd like you to replace this toaster with your top-of-the-range model. And I'd like you to pay for the repairs to the damaged plug socket, and for an entire kitchen remodel as well." If this is likely to happen, simply offer a choice of two or three more realistic options.

The same goes for children, but there's a higher chance of them asking for something totally unrealistic. A three-year-old might well insist, "I don't ever, ever want you to cook anything ever again without asking me first, even if it's for somebody else." Of course, the older they are the more reasonable they become, but only slightly. Judge their mood; you know your own children. If you're in doubt, don't give them free rein to pick the solution of their choice.

It's not generally difficult to come up with more than one route for them to choose between. For example: "What if I cooked some broccoli to pour your cheese sauce over while everyone else has macaroni? Or could you stomach macaroni-and-cheese if I make it no more than once a month?"

▶ Carry out the solution

BUSINESS TIP:

> *If you say you'll do something, you'd better make sure you do it, and do it right; otherwise, you'll blow all the good work you've just done, and your customer will be twice as angry as she was last time, and justifiably so. Be sure to check that the toaster is repaired properly if that's the option the customer picks, and make sure it's returned to her promptly and in proper working order this time.*

You don't need me to tell you what will happen if you serve your eight-year-old macaroni-and-cheese again next week. If you say you'll do something, you'd better make sure you remember. Don't commit yourself in the first place to anything you can't promise to fulfill. You may have a sneaking suspicion that she doesn't really mind macaroni-and-cheese that much anyway, but she does mind you treating her as though she's so unimportant that you can't remember your promises to her.

It should be clear by now that handling complaints for children is just the same as handling complaints for customers, whether it's a meal they don't like, or whether you always make them sit in the middle of the back seat of the car, or whether you promised you'd mend their dollhouse and still haven't.

There's only one significant difference between customers and children when it comes to complaints: ninety-six percent of unhappy customers don't bother to complain. If only children were the same!

TWO

Selling Tips

Customer relations makes sense, but selling? Why do you need selling skills to bring up children? Well, it's true that they're not likely to be in the market for any products or services you sell at work—and if they were, it would be your money they'd be spending anyway. You certainly do need to be able to sell them ideas, however.

It's not money you want them to part with, of course—that would be too easy. No, this is far more of a challenge. You want them to cooperate with you. You want to sell them the idea of eating their breakfast, or having their room painted blue instead of flourescent pink, or getting in the car to go to the store.

Selling an idea is no different from selling a product or a service. If you're used to writing proposals or giving presentations, both of which aim to sell ideas, you'll know that it's the same thing in essence. Certainly the techniques that work are the same ones. The good news is that they work just as well on children as they do on customers.

The only thing that differs is the idea you're trying to sell. You don't often find yourself selling a customer the idea of finishing up his main course completely before he can have any dessert, as you would a child. Also, children aren't necessarily as difficult to sell ideas to as adults are. You'd probably find it much harder to sell a customer the idea of fishing for leeches by holding his arms underwater in a stagnant pond until the leeches stick to them. This is an opportunity some children would jump at without hesitation.

Selling is selling, and whether it's children or customers, it pays to follow the same basic principles.

Set objectives

BUSINESS TIP:

> Before you launch into a sale, you need to know what you're trying to achieve, or how will you know if you've been successful? If you manufacture nails and screws to sell to hardware retailers, you won't be happy if you sell just three nails. You'll be aiming to sell, for example, fifteen boxes. If you sell grand country houses, on the other hand, you'll be happy simply to sell the idea of taking a look around at some houses. Whichever it is, set your objective before you start.

Children are very good at arguing you out of things—or at least trying to—or simply wearing you down. Unless you're very certain of what you're trying to achieve before you start, you have no hope of achieving it by the end of the arguing and procrastinating and the general resistance. You do have one advantage when it comes to selling to children, however. At least you know when you're going to have to work hard to make a sale. (As a general rule of thumb, the answer is always.) This means that at least you have an opportunity to prepare.

The first stage of preparation is to establish firmly in your own mind what it is that you intend to achieve. You need to be realistic, of course. A jumbo jet salesperson doesn't expect to clinch the deal on twenty-five airplanes at the first meeting with the buyer. Likewise, you can't expect to get your child to tidy his room, change the bed, do all his homework, have a bath, and be sitting at the table ready to eat when you put dinner on it. On a bad day, you can't even expect one of these things. Be sensible in your objective.

Once you've set your objective, you must hold unwaveringly to it, otherwise your children will know they've got the better of you. Once they know that's possible, they won't rest until they get the better of you next time and every time. Suppose the kids are getting fractious and irritable because they've been cooped up in the house all morning. Your objective might be: Calm them down by getting everyone to go out for the afternoon (no matter what, or you'll go mad).

Prepare alternatives

BUSINESS TIP:

> *Of course, you may not manage to sell what you hoped, but that doesn't mean the encounter with the customer has to be a dead loss. Make sure you have prepared a fallback position. If you can't sell fifteen boxes of nails at full price, you'd settle for fifteen boxes at a discount. If you can't get an appointment to view a property, at least you can get the customer to agree to look at a brochure about the property. If you're smart, you'll have a hierarchy of objectives: sell fifteen boxes, or sell ten boxes, or sell five, or leave a sample and make a follow-up appointment.*

Perhaps you think it would be a good idea to get all the kids out to the park for the afternoon so they can burn off some of that excess energy, and you won't have to do too much yourself. Maybe sit on a bench and keep an eye on them (who are you kidding?). That's your top choice for calming them down and relieving your stress, but it's not the only option that would meet your objective. And if it meets resistance, you'll need other options at the ready. Otherwise, the choice will be either to give in (and be seen to give in) by staying at home, or to physically drag them to the park if necessary, neither of which is desirable.

Make life easy on yourself. Line up some other possibilities that still meet your overall objective. Maybe you could sell the children on the idea of taking the dog for a walk, or you could even go shopping. Shopping is harder work for you, but there's more opportunity for bribing them into behaving well.

Ask open-ended questions

BUSINESS TIP:

> When you're trying to make a sale, you want the customer to do most of the talking. You need to find out what he wants from the product and what would be the plus and minus points, before you can know what to offer him. Collect information by asking questions, such as, "What size house would you be looking for? How many bedrooms?" Show you're listening to the answers by commenting or nodding.

Many parents make the mistake at this point of simply announcing what's going to happen: "Okay, everyone, we're off to the park now," which you might as well follow up by saying, "Right, everyone. I've backed myself into a corner now." Even if you're happy to walk the dog, it's going to look like backing down if you agree to it now.

Of course, there are times when there isn't a choice, or much of a choice. You can still approach the sale by asking questions. For one thing, it makes the children feel that they have had a say in the final outcome. For another thing, it gives you ammunition for making the prospect sound more attractive.

That's the real point of asking questions. When you ask a customer what he is looking for, you do it so that you can tailor your offer to his exact requirements. If you sell nails and screws, you're obviously not going to end up offering him a box of hammers and two dozen staple guns. Your choice of questions will keep the conversation within the relevant limits.

What questions are you going to ask your children? Well, the ones you want the answers to, basically. "Does anyone fancy going out?" "Where would you like to go?" "How about playing on the swings?" "Would you like to take Rover for a walk?" Gauge your questions according to the answers you get. Don't mention shopping if you think you can get away without it, but bring it into play if it looks necessary. You're using their answers to assess what is your most likely chance of a sale. Is the customer more likely to want the six-inch nails or the four-inch ones? Are the kids more likely to agree to go to the park or to take the dog out?

It's possible that the kids might all respond instantly with, "Oh, yes, the park would be great. Please, please take us to the park, and we promise to be good all day long." Then again, maybe you live in the real world. Either way, asking questions can only help you to judge where your best prospects of a sale are, rather than launching straight into it without finding out what your customer wants first.

Keep control

BUSINESS TIP:

Some customers seem to take over the sales conversation and end up cross-examining you about your products or services. You: "What kind of property are you looking for?" Customer: "What sort of properties have you got?" You: "We sell at the top end of the market, luxury country houses." Customer: "How many have you got on your books at the moment?" You: "About twelve." Customer: "Is that all?" Now, who is in charge of that conversation? You can keep control by answering any questions with a question of your own. Customer: "What sort of properties have you got?" You: "What price range are you interested in?"

It's true that customers sometimes take over a sales conversation, but at least they observe common courtesies. Children, on the other hand, feel no such compunction. They are much more likely to try to take over and railroad you into an alternative option of their choice. They'll start whining, "Why can't we stay here?" and "If you want us to go out, why don't we all go to the movies?"

Once in a while, they will inadvertently come out with a suggestion that you are perfectly happy with. If this happens, don't miss your chance. Say a brief prayer of thanks and grab the opportunity—it doesn't happen often. It's like a customer walking in and saying, "You've got some nice properties in your portfolio. I'll take this one. Oh, and I'll have this one as well."

More often, they will challenge your questions with their own: "Why the park?" In that case, simply respond with a ques-

"Don't view it as a tattoo.
Think of it as supporting the arts!"

tion of your own so that you keep control of the conversation. For example, "Don't you like the park?" If they say "no," ask them, "What don't you like about it?" You may not be getting their agreement yet; that bit comes later. For now, you're collecting information. If they say they don't like the swings, that still gives you the option of going over to the river on the other side of the park. If they've become allergic to grass since this morning, however, the trip to the park is out of the running.

Sell benefits, not features

BUSINESS TIP:

Tell the customer what your product can do for him, not simply what it is. You want to say more than "The dining room measures twenty feet by fifteen feet." Try, "The dining room is very large, so there's plenty of room to entertain your friends and family." Always express any feature of the product or service in terms of the benefits it will bring to the customer.

Children are even more self-centered than customers. It's not their fault, it's just the way they see the world. Very small children actually believe that the world revolves around them. That's why, instead of saying, "Look at the moon!" a two-year-old will often say, "The moon's looking at me!" It's not just a figure of speech, it's what they actually believe. It takes children about eighteen years to grow out of this (that's a minimum), so it's no surprise that even much older children see the world from their own perspectives.

If you want to persuade your five-year-old to go to the park—or to do anything else—it's not going to work unless she knows what's in it for her. It's no good saying, "There's plenty of fresh air at the park," or "It will occupy most of the afternoon fairly painlessly." Put it in terms that a five-year-old can relate to: "Your dolls could do with a walk in the fresh air," or "You can see how fast you can get the merry-go-round to spin without falling off," or "We might see the squirrels again, like we did last time."

Talking in terms of benefits and not features really isn't difficult. You simply have to put yourself in your child's shoes. It's as easy with a fifteen-year-old as it is with a five-year-old. Suppose you want your teenager to tidy his room: "You'll get your allowance if you do it," or "There'll be much more space for your body jewelry collection if you clear the desk," or even, to get right inside the mind of what appeals to a teenager, "I'll stop nagging you when you do it."

Handle objections

BUSINESS TIP:

> *However well you sell a product, a service, or an idea, your customer may still have reservations about it. It's too expensive, delivery will take too long, the color isn't right, or something else. You need to be able to respond to these objections in a way that will persuade the customer that they are unfounded, or at least that they are outweighed by the benefits.*

There are three things to do in handling objections.
▶ Get the customer to be specific.
▶ Put the objection into context.
▶ Give compensating factors.

▶ Get the customer to be specific

BUSINESS TIP:

> *Get your customer to make his objection as specific as possible (in other words, know your enemy). Ask him, "How much did you expect to pay?" or "How quickly do you need it?"*

If (or should I say, when) your child objects to your proposal, you can't just cave in. You could switch from suggesting to ordering—or even threatening—but the tone of the encounter will change for the worse, and the next hour or two could be unpleasant to live through. It is far better to find a way to counter the objection. When your five-year-old says, "I don't like going to the park," get her to be more specific. Ask, "What don't you like about it?"

Once you know what you're dealing with, things are much easier. The younger she is, the more true this is. Very small children sometimes have the most unexpected reasons for objecting, and you have no chance of guessing what they are. Perhaps one of the trees is in a shape that looks like a scary face, or maybe she once saw a dog in the park that barked and made her jump. No, you can't possibly know what you're up against if you don't ask.

You might believe that your child thinks the swings are boring, and she would rather stay home and play or watch television. If you ask her, however, you may get a different answer altogether, such as, "It's a very long walk to get there." That's fine—we can deal with that, now that we know what the problem is.

▶ Put the objection into context

BUSINESS TIP:

> Show the customer why, viewed in the context, the problem isn't so great: "Remember that the price includes delivery and installation costs," or "We build it to order, and then test it rigorously, so three weeks is pretty swift, if you think about it."

Your child is probably right—it probably is a long walk to the park (at least to her). You can't show her she's got the facts wrong. What you need to do is put the length of the walk in context: "It's about ten minutes each way, but we'll stay for a couple of hours. That means we'll spend most of the time playing in the park."

This works for just about anything. Let's take your reluctant teenager who doesn't want to tidy his bedroom. If you ask him why not, and he tells you it's so boring, try saying, "Parts of it are boring, but you'll find all sorts of interesting things under the bed and down the back of the chair cushions. You might even find that CD you lost a couple of weeks ago." (Whatever you do, resist the temptation to point out that it's much less boring than sitting around doing nothing, which is how he spends the rest of his free time if he's a normal teenager.)

▶ Give compensating factors

BUSINESS TIP:

> You can extend the compensations beyond the immediate context to other factors: "It's not the cheapest on the market, I grant you, but it will last you much longer than a cheaper version [context]. And you'll be the envy of your neighbors [compensating factor]."

Don't limit yourself to pointing out directly relevant factors that compensate. That's just the first stage, to address the immediate objection. Once you've done that, round it off by pointing out all the other benefits as well. You can tell your child, "It's about ten minutes each way, but we'll stay for a couple of hours. So we'll spend most of the time playing in the park, *and you can try out that new jungle gym they've just built.*"

As for your teenager, you can say, "Parts of it are boring, but you'll find all sorts of interesting things under the bed and down the back of the chair cushions. *And once you've helped me with Friday's shopping as well as tidying your room, you'll have earned yourself an extra five dollars.*"

Close the sale

BUSINESS TIP:

> Closing the sale with a customer is all about getting her to say "yes." This can mean handing over the cash, signing the contract, submitting the purchase order, or simply shaking on the deal. If you've laid the groundwork properly, as we saw earlier, you will already have made the offer or product appealing and dealt with any objections your customer may have had. All you need to do now is get her to commit herself. Customers often need prompting to do this because they are waiting for you to take the initiative, or perhaps because they are just nervous about committing to the budget in case the boss thinks they've made a stupid decision.

Children don't usually care what the boss (in other words, you) thinks, and they have no qualms about overspending budgets if they think they can get away with it. They resist for other reasons. Most often, if you've laid the groundwork well, the problem is that, although you've convinced them in principle, your timing and theirs don't agree. Just because it's worth it to tidy his bedroom and help with the shopping in exchange for extra allowance doesn't mean that your teenager wants to do either one now.

If your child happens to be two, bad luck. Two-year-olds (as you may know) think many things are a good idea, but they never want to stop what they're doing at the moment. They have a "jam tomorrow" mentality—they'll do something different tomorrow and something different yesterday, but they'll never do anything different today. However, if the shopping needs doing now because you're out of milk, bread, and even Spaghetti-O's, you need your child to agree to get in the car now and not tomorrow.

These are four of the top techniques for closing the sale, along with guidelines on how to apply them to your own children. If any of these techniques doesn't work, you haven't necessarily failed. Just make sure there are no outstanding objections and then try another technique. Pick from among the assumptive close, the alternative close, the question close, and the puppy dog close.

▶ The assumptive close

BUSINESS TIP:

This is a very simple approach—just take the sale for granted. In business terms this means saying, "That'll be $12.99 then," for example, or "I'll put you down for three green ones in the large size. Could you just sign here, please?"

When it comes to children, the key to this technique is timing. You've been through the selling process, and you've dealt with any objections; now get in there fast before they have time to notice that you're closing the deal. The second they have

"Can I take it your answer is 'yes'?"

implied agreement, or run out of objections, grab your opportunity. Don't wait for them to say "yes" or make whatever other noises children use to indicate assent.

Once you've persuaded your reluctant teenager (with or without the use of some incentive) that he should be doing more of the household chores, simply say, "I'll draw up a schedule, and then you can check it to make sure it's fair." Now leave the room quickly. You may not have won the war (what are the chances, frankly, that he'll think it's a fair schedule?), but you have won the battle. It is now taken as a given that he will do more chores; you're down to discussing details.

▶ The alternative close

BUSINESS TIP:

> A nice easy one this is. Assume the customer wants the product and just ask, "Do you want it in red or blue?" or "Do you want to take twenty this time, or would you like to start with ten?" In other words, give the customer options which don't allow him to say "no" to the purchase.

This works with children of any age, but it works particularly well with small children. It's a form of railroading, although, of course, that's not something that you'd ever do to your children, is it? Perhaps it's better to see it as giving them a choice. That is a large part of the reason why it works with small children: they like to feel that they have some control over their lives, and this technique gives it to them.

The only thing is, you're controlling the options even as they are genuinely making the final choice. Instead of saying to your four-year-old, "Put your shoes on, we're going to the park," you let her choose where to go, from a selection which you have already edited: "We're going out. Would you like to go to the park or take the dog for a walk?" Whichever she chooses, the point is that she has agreed to go out.

Since small children can be perverse, a useful variation on this technique involves making out that you have a preferred option. They will take great delight in choosing to go to the park after your mock protestations of "Please don't make me go all the way to the park; choose dog walking, please." If you actually have a preference, you can try this technique and hope your child will humor you. (By the way, this variation will not go on working through the age of eighteen. They'll see through it before then.)

▶ The question close

BUSINESS TIP:

> *Use this in response to a question, when the question appears to represent any outstanding objections. If a customer asks, "Do you have it in black?" you reply, "You'd like it in black, would you?" When she says "yes," she has effectively agreed to the sale.*

One of the advantages of this approach is that even when your children come to recognize it, they still have to go along with it. It is a sort of variation on "when did you stop beating your wife." In fact, if your child doesn't want you to use this technique on him, he will have to avoid asking the initial question in the first place. Once he has—and you've learned to spot the moment—he is caught in a trap of his own making. If he asks you a suitable question, he plays straight into your hands.

The key is recognizing your opportunity and pouncing on it. Here are a couple of examples of the kind of questions children can scuttle themselves with, and the responses you can use to clinch the deal:

"Can I go on the swings at the park?"

"Do you want to go to the park if you can go on the swings?"

"If I have to be home early, can Emily come back to stay for the night?"

"If Emily comes back with you, do you promise to be home by ten?"

▶ The puppy dog close

BUSINESS TIP:

> The name of this technique for closing the sale becomes obvious once you know how it works. It operates on the principle of "try it, and if you don't like it you can always change your mind," as in "Just take this cute little puppy home for a week, and if you don't want him after that, you can bring him back." It is the basis of the "30 days free trial" type of selling.

This works if you're sure your child will enjoy something, but you can't quite persuade her of it in advance. It's a good one to use on your two-year-old who never wants to do anything other than what he is doing already. Try saying, "We'll just go to the park for ten minutes and if you don't want to stay after that, we'll come home."

It works well on older children, too, who recognize a certain fairness in it (compared with "Just DO IT!"). It makes them feel that you're giving them ultimate control, so long as they make this little concession of trying it out for a bit first. The only thing is, you have to stick to your side of it. If they really don't like it once they've tried it, you have to accept "no" for an answer. Otherwise, they won't trust you next time, and you won't be able to use the technique again.

Selling to children is great practice for selling to customers. The techniques are the same, but you're playing for higher stakes. For one thing, children are more honest. A customer might say, "Thanks, but I don't think I will," whereas children will tell you exactly what they think of your idea if you haven't sold it well. What's more, the worst that can happen if it goes wrong with a customer is that you lose a sale. If you fail to sell an idea to your kids, instead of an afternoon in the park, you could have to spend the next four hours playing "Ken and Barbie go to the mall."

THREE

Negotiating Tips

Now, here's a collection of skills we all recognize as being important when it comes to children. There are times as a parent when family life seems to be one long round of negotiations (commonly termed "arguments"). The older children get, the less responsive they become to being told to go do something without debate. An eighteen-month-old might happily eat whatever you put in front of him, but a six-year-old is likely to launch into a lengthy bartering session about exactly how much salad he has to eat before he is allowed a bowl of ice cream for dessert.

Negotiating is often seen as a more specialized business skill than, say, good customer relations or even selling. But, in fact, all the guidelines for successful negotiating are simple to follow even if you haven't formally learned them before. As soon as you understand them, you realize that most negotiating is about psychology.

One of the most important psychological aspects of negotiation is that you need to keep your bargaining tools under your hat. You want to keep the other side in the dark about what you're prepared to settle for, or what concessions you're prepared to make. Otherwise, they'll beat you down and give you nothing in return. Reveal as little as possible and always try to find out as much as you can about their bargaining position—it's all valuable ammunition.

Negotiating is about trying to get what you want at the least cost, but in business the aim is always to do it in an atmosphere of pleasant civility. You might moan and groan privately about the opposition; in direct dealing you always strive to be polite and friendly. Occasionally this breaks down and, when it does, it hampers the negotiation. More often, there is a genuine willingness to please. The other side, after all, is only doing the same thing you are—trying to get the best deal possible.

Where children are involved, the aim should be the same. As soon as tempers start to flare, your child will develop a strong desire not only to get what he wants from the negotiation, but also to get the upper hand in the process. Since children are natural negotiators (as you already know), there is a good chance they will succeed. At the very least, you probably won't get what you want from the deal. Keep things agreeable as far as you can, for your own sake and for the sake of reaching a workable negotiated solution with your child.

Negotiate a win-win deal

BUSINESS TIP:

Everyone goes into a negotiation wanting to clinch a good deal, which is often at the expense of the other side. In other words, a person will treat it as a battle, the object of which is winning. The trick is to make your opponent feel he's won, while also coming out feeling that you've won. It's known as win-win negotiating. The way to do it is to ask for more than you want (or offer less than you really intend), and then let your opponent beat you to the level you were expecting to settle for all along. The other side thinks it's won, but you've got exactly what you want, too. You've both won.

Most children have healthy egos, and they don't want to lose face. If your negotiation tactics leave them feeling they've lost, and it shows, they are unlikely to come to an agreement. Then you're back to enforcing the rule of law, which is far less effective. Negotiated agreements are better than enforced submissions for several reasons.

▶ They avoid stressful and unpleasant encounters.
▶ Everyone feels successful and positive.

▸ The agreement has the support of both sides, so you are both much more likely to stick to it.

Of course, there aren't enough hours in the day to enter full-scale negotiations over every little thing, right down to whether kids should get dressed before or after they brush their teeth. Neither should there be any call to. The win-win approach is useful in the briefest of informal negotiations, when your child doesn't even realize he's negotiating at all.

Suppose your nine-year-old child asks to play with his new toy after supper, instead of going straight to bed. If you're smart, you'll decide how long an extension he can have, and then offer him less in order to give him room to win a negotiation. So you say, "Okay, but only ten minutes." He says (as you knew he would), "Oh, please, can I have twenty minutes?" You can then settle for twenty, or even meet in the middle at fifteen. Either way, you've just held a successful win-win negotiation in the space of a few seconds.

In order to come up with a win-win solution, you have to be able to look at the problem from the child's point of view. The odds are that your child will be more than happy to fill you in on the way he sees things. You must make an effort to appreciate it, rather than simply hear him out because you feel you should. If you really understand things from his side, you are likely to be more willing to make concessions.

Imagine that your fourteen-year-old daughter wants to go out to a dance and come back at half past eleven at night on the bus. You think this is far too late for her to be out, and going by bus is an unsafe way to travel (especially given what she'll probably want to wear). But listen to her point of view: all her friends will be there, and she'll feel really stupid if she's the only one whose parents won't let her go.

Come on. Don't you remember being fourteen? It's humiliating when your parents won't let you join in with what everyone else is doing. You still may not agree to the arrangements as they stand, but once you see her point of view, don't you feel more inclined to cooperate? Wouldn't you like her to feel that she's won an agreement from you that she's happy with?

"Wow, we tricked Mom into buying us a DVD player if we just get A's on our report cards!"

Why not let her go to the dance, but make the finish time a little earlier? You could also pick her up in the car. You've got what you want—you feel that she's safe, and she's got what she wants—she gets to go to the dance. Both of you leave the negotiation feeling successful.

There's just one essential rule for win-win negotiating with your children: you must never, ever let them know your technique. Their satisfaction lies in thinking that you've lost, you've got egg all over your face, and they've handled the negotiation better than you. If you ever let them find out that none of these is actually the case, you will have thrown away one of their biggest incentives to reach a mutual agreement—the satisfaction of beating you. (Well, maybe they're not that vengeful, but they do like to feel that they too have power.) So keep it to yourself. When they've grown up, left home, and entered the world of business, they may finally learn the rules of negotiating and recognize your tactics. By then it won't matter anymore.

Know your bottom line

BUSINESS TIP:

In every negotiation, there is a theoretical point below which the deal stops being worthwhile. Suppose you're negotiating to sell a great many of your products to a customer for a bulk discount. You've done your figures, and you know that you'd be happy to give him a ten percent discount, but you'd settle for fifteen. More than twenty percent, however, and the deal just isn't worth having. Therefore, twenty percent is your absolute bottom line.

If you go into a deal without knowing your bottom line, there is nothing to stop your child from bargaining you down to the point where the deal just isn't worth it. If you haven't set your bottom line, you won't recognize this point. Sooner or later, of course, you'll realize you've stepped beyond it, but by then it will be too late.

Suppose your twelve-year-old is haggling with you for a later bedtime. You're suggesting nine o'clock, but she thinks it should be half past ten. Before you know where you are, you've agreed to ten o'clock. After you've had a chance to think about it, you're really not happy with this at all. However, there's nothing you can do about it. Do you really want to go back and tell your twelve-year-old that you're reneging on the agreement? And do you honestly think that you have a chance of getting away with it? As far as children are concerned, a deal is a deal—at least when it's in their favor.

The thing to do is to decide before you start negotiating exactly how late is the latest you'll agree to. Maybe it's half past nine. In the interests of win-win negotiating, you can start by offering nine o'clock. That way, your child will feel she's won when you finally agree to half past nine. Who knows, she might even settle for nine o'clock without fussing (and pigs might fly).

And what, you might be wondering, are you supposed to do when you have to think on your feet? A smart child springs these negotiations on you when you least expect it because she knows her chances of success are better if she catches you by surprise. She waits until you're preoccupied helping her little brother with his homework while also getting supper ready, feeding the dog, and preparing the packed lunches for school tomorrow. Then she nonchalantly inquires, "Don't you think it's time my bedtime was a bit later? All my friends go to bed at about half past ten." You're supposed to say, "Do they, darling? Oh, fair enough then."

No, no, no! She is getting the better of you. Even if you've got the sense to argue the case rather than simply capitulating, this won't do. If a customer called you in the middle of a meeting and started trying to negotiate a deal with you, you'd say, "I'm in a meeting at the moment, and I can't give this the attention it deserves. Can I call you back this afternoon?" Or even, "Can I call you later and make an appointment to come see you so we can discuss it?"

Follow the same tactic with your child. Say, "Sorry, but I'm very busy at the moment. Let's talk about it later, when I can give you my full attention." That should stop her little game, while sounding completely cooperative and willing to negotiate. Wait until you can talk on your own terms. Now you've bought time to sit down and think through the issue, and you can decide what your bottom line is before negotiations begin.

You may not need to fix a bottom line for tiny, everyday negotiations, such as whether or not the kids have to eat everything on their plates (though once you get into the habit, it comes quickly and naturally even for these small deals). To make sure the results of the agreement are going to last into the future, such as with bedtime, allowance, or anything that sets a precedent, always know your bottom line before you agree to start talking.

Remember these two important points about your bottom line.

- Never let the opponent—your children—find out what your bottom line is. Otherwise, they won't settle for anything less.
- Never claim to have reached your bottom line unless you have, or you'll be crying wolf. If you say, "That's absolutely as far as I can go," you'd better mean it. If you let them beat you down further, they won't believe you next time you say it, even if it's true.

Aim high

BUSINESS TIP:

A successful negotiation depends on having room to maneuver. If neither of you is prepared to budge from your starting positions, you haven't got the basis for a negotiation at all. Your room to maneuver is the space between what you start off asking for and the bottom line you'd be prepared to settle for. The higher you aim initially, the more scope for negotiating you have . . . and the better chance that you will never have to drop as low as your bottom line. If you can afford an absolute maximum discount of twenty percent, don't start by offering eighteen percent. Start with ten percent and give yourself plenty of negotiating room.

Let's say your son's seventh birthday is coming up, and he wants to invite all his school friends to a big party. Your personal preference is to take him out for a treat on his own. Or, failing that,

"My bedtime just got moved to third shift!"

to get someone else to host the party so that you can leave the country for a few hours. You're going to have to negotiate how many friends he can invite.

You'll have to think about this one first, and decide what your bottom line is. Perhaps you feel you can just about cope with eight of the rascals running around for the afternoon. But you can't start by offering him eight, or you have no room to give any ground—and that's not a negotiation. Besides, just because you can stand eight doesn't mean you wouldn't be happier with six.

Aim high. If you can, find out how many kids he wants to invite (he may be too unpracticed at negotiating to avoid revealing this information). You often tend to meet in the middle on this kind of deal, so if you know how many he wants, you can try to make sure eight is the middle point. If he has a list of ten, you can stipulate a maximum of six. Then you can meet in the middle at eight. If his list has twelve names on it and you start out by saying six, you can't arrive at eight unless he gives more ground than you do. How easy will that be to negotiate? If he wants twelve, you can start at four. If you give other concessions too (as we'll see later), you might end up with even fewer than eight.

Yes, I realize that if he wants to invite twenty friends then this system isn't going to be foolproof. However, the odds are that he knows perfectly well that twenty is unrealistic. As we'll see, there are other variables you can bring into play. If you have no idea how many people he wants to invite, and you can't wheedle a figure out of him, simply aim high. Suggest he invites his two or three closest friends, and be prepared to give a fair bit of ground if you have to.

Remember that you need to start by aiming high, because once you've agreed to lower your demands, you can't raise them again. Imagine saying to an employee in the middle of negotiating a pay raise, "Sorry, but actually I can't offer you that five percent pay raise I said I could, after all. Three percent is my absolute limit." It's just not going to work. If you don't ask for it to begin with, you've no chance of getting it later. You can't promise your son seven friends at his party and then reduce it to four later. Your life wouldn't be worth living.

The one remaining question is: how high should you aim? The answer is simple: as high as you can justify. If you ask your boss to budget five extra staff to help you cover the exhibition next month, you know that you have to be able to justify why you need five rather than only three or four. Well, the same goes here. How few friends can you justify allowing your son to invite? Think about other parties he's been to, or what he wants this party to entail, and decide the minimum you can offer.

It's the same with your twelve-year-old's bedtime. You'll have a hard time justifying a bedtime of half past six, but consider when her older siblings go to bed, what time she has to get up in the morning, what time she goes to bed now, and come up with the earliest bedtime you can reasonably justify. You're being kind, really, you're giving her the chance to beat you even more.

Look for variables

BUSINESS TIP:

If you have only one factor to consider, such as money, you're not really negotiating at all. You're haggling. You offer to sell for twelve thousand dollars, the customer counters with ten thousand dollars, you suggest eleven thousand dollars, and it's a deal. A negotiation is more subtle and complex because you can bring in other factors, or variables. Suppose a supplier says eleven thousand dollars, and you say you'll give him eleven if he can deliver the product within three weeks. Now you're juggling cost and delivery time, and you're into a true negotiation. The more of these variables you can find, the more bargaining levers you have.

It's always worth bringing in as many variables as you can to a negotiation, especially if you haven't much room to maneuver on the central point at issue. If bedtime is currently nine o'clock and you're really not prepared to move far on it at all, it will help if you can introduce other factors. Maybe you can offer a later bedtime on weekends and holidays, or perhaps you could let the kids leave the light on until ten o'clock. Or, let them have one late night each week if there's a particular television program they want to watch. You could even offer to throw in a new set of more grown-up bedding (covered in a sports motif rather than elephants).

No doubt your children will be able to come up with plenty of suggestions of their own if you ask them, especially once they recognize that you won't shift beyond a certain time for going to bed. They'll feel that they're getting concessions from you, and you'll get to find out what will work best as an incentive to get them to reach an agreement.

You can be as creative as you like. As long as you can make offers that will appeal to your children, any variable factor like this can help to clinch a deal. If you have both reached your bottom line and still haven't met in the middle, variables can be the only way to find a workable solution. The thing is, the variables can influence the bottom line. You're still set on nine o'clock bedtime, but it doesn't have to apply on weekends. The kids still want to go to bed at ten, but might concede four out of five weekdays.

One of the advantages of variables is that they often help you to avoid ever reaching your bottom line. With no other bargaining points in play, you might have to let your seven-year-old push you into letting him invite eight friends to his party. Introduce variables into the negotiation, and you may well keep him to fewer. For example, one of these might work.

▸ For every person he knocks off his invitation list, you'll add twenty dollars to the budget for the party (if you're going to use bribery, you might as well be creative with it).
▸ If there are no more than two friends (let him negotiate you up to three here), you'll take them all out for a special treat, such as to the circus or a movie.
▸ The fewer the party guests, the longer the party can go on (put it this way to be positive, rather than saying that the more there are, the shorter it will have to be).
▸ He can have eight people on the condition that none of them is either Jim or Matt, each of whom counts as two people (and that's being conservative).

Anything that will help you to reach an agreement is okay. It doesn't have to have anything to do with the matter under negotiation, so long as you are both prepared to bargain with it. So, you might say that if he limits the number of friends he invites, you'll have his bike repainted the color he wants.

You can be endlessly creative with variables once you get into practice. Here's another standard negotiation that all of us have to hold with our children sooner or later: allowance. Instead of simply haggling, think of some more variables.

- Half of their allowance money is sacrosanct and the other half has to be earned by doing chores.
- They can't have the raise they want, but you'll give them a book allowance every month as well.
- Allowance can go up, but they have to save a percentage of it towards more expensive items that you approve of (they can always save the rest of it towards things you don't approve of).
- Allowance can go up and responsibilities will go up, too.

The choices are unlimited. You have far more scope when it comes to negotiating with your children than with your customers or your boss because you should have a much better idea of what will motivate them, even if it's unrelated to the subject under discussion. After all, you can't generally sway a customer by saying, "Oh, and if you'll settle for a fifteen percent discount, I'll take you camping on Saturday night."

Get all the cards on the table

BUSINESS TIP:

Some people go into negotiations with the intention of being underhanded and tricking you into giving away more than you meant to. The classic technique for doing this is to wait until you've almost agreed to the deal, and then throw something new onto the table. Perhaps you've already said that you can give them a fifteen percent discount, and then they announce that they also need delivery within a week. It's too late to use this as a bargaining lever because you've committed to the dis-

> count. The way to prevent this is to agree to a list of factors at issue before you begin. That way, they can't reasonably introduce anything new at the last minute. If they do, you can refuse to discuss it without going back over other factors.

I'm sure your child is an honest, fair-minded, open person who would be horrified at the mere thought of employing any kind of underhanded tactics. Well, maybe with someone else, but parents are different—they're fair game. Your child can get all her Machiavellian tendencies out of her system on you so that everyone else can get the benefit of the honest, decent side of her nature. Everyone, that is, except you—you, who did all the hard work of making her fair and honest in the first place.

Face it. When she is negotiating with you, your child can be as underhanded, cheating, and manipulative as everyone else's. It's only a matter of time before she works out (if she hasn't already) that the smart way to get what she wants is to conceal half her demands until you've all but agreed to the first half. Even if you feel you haven't committed yourself yet, you've still revealed what you're prepared to settle for.

Don't tell your seven-year-old that he can have six people at his party, and then have him announce that he wants to take everyone to the movies. If you'd known that, you'd have limited the numbers to three or four. You will often find that if you think about it, you can work out what many of your child's demands are likely to be. You could have guessed, really, that your son would have wanted to discuss the nature of the party.

The answer is to treat your child as you would a customer or employee whom you were negotiating with. Begin by saying, "Let's make a list of everything that both of us want to talk about with allowance" (or whatever is at issue) "so we can make sure that we both know where we are, and we won't miss anything important."

You will have to be honest here too, of course. I'm afraid that's the price you pay for training your children to be honest. It's worth it to avoid that sinking feeling when they suddenly throw a fresh issue into the equation just as you thought you'd solved it.

"I assume my allowance doesn't include
my expense account."

What happens if, just supposing, you fail to take this precautionary step? It can happen, especially if you didn't realize until you were underway what a full-scale negotiation this would turn out to be. The danger is that you will be pressured into making an instant response that you will regret later (that was their whole point in doing it). Don't let it happen. In fact, the solution lies in one of the rules of negotiating that we'll cover later: agree to all or nothing. As you'll see, it will keep you out of the worst trouble here.

Never give free concessions

BUSINESS TIP:

If the other side wants something from you, make it clear that you expect something in return. When they say, "We'll need a bigger discount—say, fifteen percent," you don't simply agree, you make a trade-off: "We could only do that if you paid thirty percent up front." Rather than yield concessions, trade them for concessions from the other side.

If your child states what she needs and you say, "Okay," then even if it's only one of the variables and not the whole deal, you're not negotiating. You're giving in. You need to trade blow for blow (metaphorically speaking, of course) in order to clinch the outcome you want.

Do a deal on every point. When your son asks to go to the circus for his birthday party, say you can only manage that if everyone gets delivered straight home afterwards. When your daughter asks to stay up until ten on Tuesday nights to watch a favorite program, tell her she'll have to have her homework finished daily before bed, not leaving it until the morning. When you ask your teenager to tidy his room, and he offers to tidy the floor but leave his desk as it is, try saying, "You can leave the desk for now, but the leeches will have to go."

There are two reasons for trading concessions rather than giving them away. The first is that you are more likely to end up with what you need. It's the way to bring all those variables into play so that, although your daughter might now be staying up later, at least the lights are out at a sensible time, and her homework is getting done after school and not in a panicked rush at seven o'clock in the morning.

The other reason for trading concessions is a psychological one (as with so many negotiating skills). You need to show your children that you're a tough negotiator, and that they needn't bother asking you to lower your requirements unless they're prepared to give something up, too. This is even more important with children than with customers, colleagues, and bosses. After all, you are likely to be involved in negotiations with your children for years to come, with no option of changing jobs or even being promoted into a new role.

Your best bet is to earn yourself a reputation as such a tough negotiator that, unless your child is ready to compromise properly, he will choose not to negotiate with you at all but to pester his other parent instead. When that happens, you know you've got the skills of negotiating really licked.

Agree to all or nothing

BUSINESS TIP:

You wouldn't sign a contract until all the points in it were agreed upon, and you shouldn't commit yourself to any part of a negotiation until all the points are agreed upon either. As soon as you give a definite "yes" to one point, you can no longer use it to bargain with. All your variables should slide up and down on a kind of mental scale until they are all in balance—a little more money, but a better delivery time and reasonable payment terms. Juggle them all, and play them off against each other, until they fit. If you lock off any one of them at a fixed, agreed point, you make the balancing act much harder, if not impossible.

Negotiating is like making a vinaigrette without a recipe. You put in a bit of oil, then a bit of vinegar, and then sugar, salt, pepper, mustard, and so on. You keep tasting it. If it's too sweet, you bump up the other ingredients to compensate. If it's not sharp enough, you add a little vinegar. If at any point you decide that you definitely aren't going to change the amount of oil in there, no matter what, you're going to be stumped if it's too vinegary. You've left yourself no room to maneuver. You need to be able to adjust all the ingredients until the dressing tastes just right.

Keep your options open regarding any of your child's requests until you both can agree to the whole deal. This is also good insurance against the problems that arise if you don't get all her cards on the table before you begin, as we discussed earlier. As you discuss each issue in the deal you will, of course, reach a preliminary agreement on each one. Simply wait to commit to it until they've all been discussed and a settlement reached. That way, you can bring an earlier issue back into play as a bargaining point if you need to.

When the question of staying up until ten o'clock on Tuesdays seems settled (or the question of where to go for the party, or the amount of allowance), say something like, "Well, that sounds workable, so let's leave it for the moment and talk about the clothes you don't wear anymore."

By the way, agreeing to parts of a deal too soon is a mistake that many experienced managers and salespeople make. You'll be practicing a valuable work skill on your child when you keep your options open with him. More to the point, you'll get the deal you want.

Once you have agreed to all the issues, balanced against each other in a way that satisfies everyone, summarize them before you finally commit—and get commitment from your child. If necessary, you can write them down between you so that you can see you're both happy with them. However you do it, make sure you're both clear on what you've agreed to: "So, you'll tidy the bedroom floor and the chairs, but you can do what you like with the desktop. You'll clear out all the trash from your room and put it out in the garbage can, and the clothes will be gone by the weekend. Every Saturday evening you can have an extra two dollars allowance if your bedroom is tidy—starting this Saturday. Are we both in agreement?"

It's also a good idea to have some agreed indicator that signifies your agreement on the deal. Just as in business you shake on a deal and then sign, so, too, at home you need to be clear when the thing is settled and negotiations are over. You might shake hands on it, or write it down and both sign the paper. Or, you might simply know because you're on speaking terms again. Whatever your system, make sure you have one so that there are no further arguments on the subject.

However tough a negotiation is, never underrate the fact that your child is negotiating at all. Nobody enters a negotiation unless they have some underlying wish to deal with you, in preference to leaving things as they are or facing your wrath. Whether it is the Middle East peace process, or just you trying to encourage your seven-year-old to brush her teeth regularly, any negotiation is better than none.

FOUR

Motivation Tips

Children can be hugely enthusiastic and positive, and are capable of putting enormous effort into projects. They just have to feel motivated. You won't need to put any effort into motivating your teenager to dye her hair purple, or your four-year-old to have a go on his new bicycle. However, motivation skills are essential if you want to get your children to do other things, such as homework or cleaning and tidying.

Managers need to motivate their staff just as you need to motivate your children. It can be a little tougher with children, though. At work, your staff know that they have to put in some effort if they want to keep their jobs, so there is a level of self-motivation even if you need to build on it. At home, your children have no such incentive. You can't fire them, and they know it. So, you sometimes find yourself faced with no motivation in your children, which you need to turn into sufficient enthusiasm to embark on a project and see it through.

A manager needs to keep firm control and be seen as a figure of authority and respect in order to get the desired performance from the team members. Using carrot rather than stick techniques to motivate team members to perform and cooperate works best and does not undermine their confidence.

How can you get your children to want to do things that they are not initially keen on? It might be cleaning out the rabbit hutch, getting their homework done, or going on vacation to somewhere you chose and they didn't. Or, it might be a more long-term issue: taking on extra chores, traveling to school on their own instead of getting a ride from you, or working harder to get good grades in biology. Whatever the issue, the selling skills we've already looked at will help. However, even if you can sell an idea to your child in the first instance, you still need to keep her eager to pursue it to the end.

Show your team the big picture

BUSINESS TIP:

Let your staff see how their jobs fit in with the whole organization. Show them what else goes on and explain how their roles mesh with it. Let them see the results of their hard work: if they make wheel bearings for the cars you manufacture, let them drive one of the finished cars.

Your children are part of the whole family, and they need to understand their place in it. You might tell them that you can't take them out on Thursday; it may be their school holiday, but you've still got to go to work. Rather than leaving it at that, explain (helpfully, without lecturing) why the whole family benefits from you working. If you can, let them come to work with you for a morning and see what you do.

Why not trade jobs with your child for a day? (You might need to modify this approach a little, especially for a small child.) Do it on a weekend when you don't have to go to work; otherwise, your boss might be a little surprised to see a smartly dressed six-year-old pulling up at the office and settling down at your computer, peering up over the screen. Get your child to cook the dinner, wash the car, do the cleaning, or whatever you do, while you do whatever it is he does on the weekend. You should have a pretty easy time of this (you're excused from hanging around the mall pointlessly for hours with a large group of fourteen-year-olds). Do his chores for him, though, before you put your feet up.

The object of the exercise is not to be able to say, "See! I work my fingers to the bone all day while you do nothing." It is to help your children see how what they do fits (or doesn't) with what everyone else does. Make it as fun as you can. If you have more than one child, let them assume collective responsibility for all of your chores, while you do all theirs.

Set clear and realistic targets

BUSINESS TIP:

> *If you want people to improve their performances, you have to agree to realistic targets for them to attain. If you don't, they don't know when they are doing well, which is a strong demotivator. For example, agree that their conversion rate of inquiries to sales should rise from twenty to twenty-five percent in the next three months, or that all brochures should be sent out within twenty-four hours of being requested.*

How often have you said to your child, "You're going to have to clean the rabbit hutch out more often," or "Your bedroom's always such a mess—do something about it," or "Stop waking us up so early in the morning. Play for a bit by yourself first"?

We all give these vague orders, but we've only ourselves to blame when nothing seems to change. The child won't clean out the rabbit hutch more often—he hasn't a clue what "more often" means. Every day? Twice a week? And there's an added implication that you're not really bothered—if you were, you'd clarify what you want to make sure it really happened.

If you want your child to improve his performance in some way, be specific. You may have to refer to the chapter on negotiating to get him to agree to some of your targets (a four-year-old won't go along with playing quietly in his bedroom until eleven o'clock every morning without a fight). Make sure that you agree to something specific.

Maybe you feel that your daughter should tidy her bedroom every Saturday morning (although the amount of garbage that can collect in a teenager's bedroom in the space of seven days might seem like more than any human could clean up in a morning. Not to mention that the entire family supply of mugs and teaspoons will have vanished into the gloom by Tuesday). Perhaps your son should start his homework by half

"Would you rather go to the dentist without a fuss and get a new CD, or skip the dentist, lose your teeth, never get a job, and live with your parents for the rest of your life?"

past five every evening. He could aim to clean out that rabbit hutch on the weekend and top off the sawdust every Wednesday. You could set an alarm for eight o'clock for your four-year-old to let her know it's okay to wake you up. (The next stage is to get her to do it by kissing you gently on the cheek instead of exploding in through the door and leaping onto the trampoline, I mean, bed, with a yell of "Wake up! NOW!")

Inform team members

BUSINESS TIP:

Always tell people what's going on in the organization as far as you can. Ask for their ideas and suggestions when problems need solving. It should go without saying that you must be perceived as listening to the answers, too, even if you don't eventually act on them. Involving people makes them feel that they have a stake in what's going on, so they care more about it. When it's a success, of course, you must acknowledge their part in it.

It's easy to leave our children out of what's going on, and then expect them to follow blindly. With small children this is especially true. We tend to stick them in the car without even telling them where we're going, and then we get annoyed if they complain when we get there. It's not really surprising that they resent being dragged off to places without a by-your-leave. How would you feel? Older children tend to ask for the information. They still feel that they're unimportant to you if they know you wouldn't have told them had they not asked.

We generally leave our children uninformed because the matter at issue has nothing to do with them, or we think they wouldn't be interested. This misses the point. Obviously, when you tell your twelve-year-old that the frumpy, middle-aged woman who's just arrived is going to measure your bedroom chair for a new cover, you hardly expect him to get overexcited about it. However, you've demonstrated that he has a right to know what's going on and, until you tell your child, who knows what he might be thinking? Perhaps he was imagining that she was a neighbor coming to complain about the loud music blaring from his bedroom, or a travel company rep coming to tell you that you've won a family holiday abroad, or an animal welfare officer coming to take away the poor, neglected rabbit.

Suppose you have a family problem. Say your children are getting old enough to have their own rooms, but you're not sure how to fit them in. Do you move to a bigger house? Divide a room in two? Add on to the house? Whatever you do, involve the children. Explain the problem, and ask them what they think. They may have an idea that you haven't thought of. "Why not convert the garage and make a bedroom downstairs?" Whether you take their advice or not, if they've been involved in the discussion, then they are far more likely to be motivated to go along with whatever solution you finally reach.

Find the right incentive

BUSINESS TIP:

> *Incentives encourage your team to meet targets that you set for them (or better yet, those you set together). Different people respond to different incentives.*

One of the best incentives is bribery. It has a bad name among parents because it feels like cheating, but that's only because we associate it with a pathetic attempt at appeasement. This doesn't have to be the case. There's a world of difference between bribing a child to say "yes" after he has initially refused, and bribing him before you start. In other words, if you anticipate trouble, you can start out by saying, "It's time to go shopping. Come on—if you're good I'll buy you an ice cream cone on the way home." This is not the same thing at all as begging your shrieking child, as he lies kicking and flailing on the floor of the supermarket, to "Please be good, and I'll buy you an ice cream cone."

Now we can stop calling these temptations bribes, and start calling them by the words we use at work: rewards, incentives, motivating factors. There. Now you don't have to feel guilty any more. You're not bribing your child, you're "incentivizing" him.

Remember to do it *before* he has misbehaved or failed to pull his weight, so that you don't reward the misbehavior.

You can always employ more than one incentive to motivate your child. Some of these incentives can work either before or after the issue in question. For example, you might motivate a freedom-loving child to do something by giving him the freedom to do it his own way. You might also motivate him by letting him know that if he cooperates, you will give him greater freedom of some other kind. Here is a rundown of the key incentives that managers use with their staff:

▶ Money, security, status, recognition, responsibility, job satisfaction, challenge, and freedom.

▶ Money

BUSINESS TIP:

You can offer your staff a raise, a bonus, or a commission if they perform well, and for many people this is the most valuable recognition of their achievements you can give.

Clearly you don't need to be told that many children respond in an extremely positive way to the prospect of money, although the kind of financial incentive that will satisfy a five-year-old won't impress a fifteen-year-old. Be inventive about how you offer money as an incentive. It doesn't have to be a question of simply handing over the cash if your child does as you ask.

Certainly you can pay your children for doing specific tasks. Arguably, it's only fair to pay them for doing a job that benefits you and not them, for example, washing your car for you. You can also offer the hope of an increase in allowance after, say, three months, if during that time they have consistently come home on time after evenings out, or have done their turn at washing up without complaint (well, without excessive complaint—let's not make it too hard for them).

One possible allowance system has two levels: a basic allowance a child gets no matter what, plus an extra sum if he has done all his chores as well that week. You can then negotiate either of these levels to go up if he carries out extra chores or adds responsibilities.

You could even find a way to make the incentive suit the situation. Suppose your teenage daughter doesn't want to clear out her closet of all the old clothes she never wears any more. Offer her the price of a new outfit for doing the job, but for every extra day it takes her to get round to doing it, you knock a few dollars off the budget.

▶ Security

BUSINESS TIP:

> Some people are particularly resistant to change and feel threatened by it. Money often represents security to these people, but so do other factors. Financially, they would prefer a small raise over the chance of a big commission, which they might not manage to earn. They want to know where they stand. They might also be motivated by a good pension plan, or by a permanent contract rather than a freelance or consulting contract.

If you have a child who likes security and consistency, and is resistant to change, you can often motivate her by promising that in exchange for her cooperation, you will make sure that certain things don't change. Suppose you're going to convert your garage so that your children can have separate bedrooms. Persuade the one who dislikes change that if she helps with the decorating, you'll let her stay in the room she's in now. You can then find some other incentive, if you need it, to encourage the other child to move to the new room.

Never be afraid of using different incentives for each child. It might seem fair to treat all your children identically, and, of course, in some matters it is, but often it is far from fair. The same incentive has a different value for each child, and it's much fairer to offer parity of value to all your children than a superficially matching incentive.

▶ Status

BUSINESS TIP:

> Promotion is a huge incentive to people who are motivated by status, and so is a better job title, a bigger office, or a flashier company car. You could also put an employee in charge of a prestigious new project.

When you look at your three- or four-year-old, you can probably already tell if he will grow up to be easily swayed by the promise of a fancier job title. By the time he is seven or eight, you'll certainly know. Introducing job titles within the family might not be practical, and although your teenager would doubtless love his own "company" car, you might not be so keen on the idea. Nevertheless, there is still an almost limitless scope for conferring status as an incentive.

Your child will most want high status among friends and peers, so this crowd should be the source of your incentives. He will want the latest fashions, the best sports shoes, the flashiest CD player, or. whatever his friends yearn for. These are the incentives to offer in recognition of good performance. Again, if you can match the incentive to the performance, better still. If his school clothes are clean every morning when he puts them on, he can have a new pair of sports shoes at the end of the term—that sort of thing.

One word of caution about offering status incentives: don't give a child higher status than her siblings. You can give her an important job, such as being in charge of booking the family holiday (if that makes her feel important), but don't let her set the itinerary, or have the power to delegate tasks to brothers or sisters (most children will find it hard to distinguish between delegating and issuing orders—together with threats, if they see fit). You will drive a wedge between your children if you let them juggle status between them, as well as encourage family fights. Stick to status symbols that are designed to impress their friends.

"Summer school might seem like a lateral career move, but it comes with a great benefits package!"

▶ Recognition

BUSINESS TIP:

> Some people derive their greatest satisfaction in knowing that they have impressed you. They want to be appreciated. For these people, being recognized and thanked for good work will mean more than a bonus or a fancy new office (although giving them another incentive, as well as recognition, often works better than recognition alone).

Perhaps the easiest children of all to motivate are those who are eager for parental approval. If you have one of these, congratulations. She will often be happy to do something simply because you say, "I'll be really pleased if you do it," or "You'd need to be pretty grown up to do this, but I reckon you might be able to."

This kind of motivation will only work over the long term if your child knows that you will also recognize her achievement afterwards. You have to say, "Well done!" If you often fail or forget to notice when she has done well, your claims of being really impressed or pleased will start to ring hollow. Follow through and comment when she succeeds. Recognition matters more to these types of children than to others (we'll look at how to recognize people later on).

As these children grow older, it's a bit much to hope that recognition alone will motivate them every time. It may keep them going through the smaller tasks, like making you a cup of coffee at the end of the day, while their more money-motivated brother or sister is asking, "What's it worth?" They're still going to start wanting other kinds of recognition for bigger achievements, especially if they have siblings who are recognized in other ways. It's no good saying to a group of children, "Well done, all of you. To show how grateful I am, here's twenty dollars for you, a new CD for you, and a big thank-you for you."

▶ Responsibility

BUSINESS TIP:

> In some cases, the best kind of recognition you can give is added responsibility. It can make people feel important, and shows that you trust them. Whatever the reason, putting someone in charge of a project, or giving him an extra responsibility, will encourage his long-term commitment to you and to his job.

Many children like to feel grown up, and giving them more responsibility is often a great way to motivate them. If they feel important and trusted, they won't want to let you down. You can use this approach on very small children by letting them play in the yard alone (while you watch neurotically from the window), if they promise to leave the sandbox cleaned up and the hutch closed so the rabbit will stay inside. Or, tell them that if they're good in the supermarket, then they can help you pick items off the shelf or help pack the groceries into bags at the checkout counter.

Older children will often respond well to being treated like adults, being allowed to take responsibility for their own bedtime (so long as school grades don't suffer), or being able to buy their own back pack if you just give them the money. If the rising phone bill is a problem (and it's not you who's been running it up), why not give your child her own phone and a fixed budget for calls, with the bills sent to her? She'll feel responsible and trusted, and she'll also have to pay any excess charges herself.

The important thing to remember about responsibility is that it's very hard to take it away once you've given it. Therefore, if you are conferring a permanent responsibility, such as giving your child control of his own bedtime, you need him to prove that he is capable of handling the responsibility before you give it. You could start by giving him control on weekends only, or you could have a test period for two or three weeks, and a fixed review date at the end of it.

If your child doesn't come up to scratch but has clearly been trying, see if you can find a compromise settlement. Maybe you could give him a later bedtime for now, or give him control during holidays. That way, he will feel that although he didn't earn everything he wanted, at least you are recognizing the achievement he did manage.

▶ Job satisfaction

BUSINESS TIP:

> No one is going to feel satisfied if he knows he isn't doing his job well. Try to give people tasks they are well suited to, so that they will be able to feel they've made a good job of it.

This incentive works for just about everyone, and is a very useful one when you're divvying up chores if you have more than one child. It ties in with recognition, too. Your child will need to hear you say, "Well done. I knew if you were in charge of putting the garbage out, it would get done." (You don't have to add that it certainly ought to, seeing as she generates three quarters of the empty soda pop cans, pizza boxes, cookie wrappers, and the rest of the rubbish and recyclable items.)

Some children are very active, so they'd be good at changing the beds or clearing out the garage. Some like to be outdoors, so get them to mow the grass. Some like things to be organized and tidy, so they can load the dishwasher. Some fancy themselves as being mechanically minded, so put them in charge of changing light bulbs (although not if they're only four). You get the point. Give them jobs they know they're good at, and then reinforce their own feelings by telling them how well they've done the jobs.

▶ Challenge

BUSINESS TIP:

> People who enjoy a challenge are motivated by knowing that if they do a good job, you'll give them something else even tougher to sink their teeth into. They relish the idea of being given training so that they'll be able to take on more difficult tasks in the future.

14 • *Family Matters*

"I understand the position of Lawn Care Specialist is open. Here's my resume."

A child who relishes a challenge will be happy to take on most responsibilities or tasks that she thinks will test her skills. Get her to figure out how the new video recorder works, or make her responsible for drawing up the weekly shopping list. You can encourage small children of this type to learn new skills, such as getting themselves dressed in the morning, simply for the challenge of it.

The downside of motivating this kind of child is that she is often the most resistant to any chore that poses no challenge at all. Getting her to wash the dishes or tidy her room can be pretty difficult. You might have to clean out the rabbit hutch for her in exchange for her setting the video timer for you.

▶ Freedom

BUSINESS TIP:

> *Some workers, often the less orthodox types, particularly enjoy personal freedom. They are often motivated by being put in charge of their own time, or being allowed to work from home or on some kind of flextime. They may also like tasks that give them plenty of opportunities to get out of the office more often.*

If you have one of those children who is naturally resentful of authority, you can have trouble getting him to do anything. Even if you wield your authority with kindness and respect, he will resent it simply because it's there at all. The more control you can relinquish to him over his own life, the happier he will be.

Rather than ask this kind of a child to clean out the rabbit hutch on a Saturday morning, just say you want it done by Sunday night. Let him choose his own time over the weekend to do it. Put your small child's food in a serving dish beside her own plate and let her help herself, rather than presenting her with a *plate accompli*. You'll have far fewer arguments over what she will and won't eat. The more freedom you allow these kinds of children in carrying out the task, the more willing they will be to do it.

When it comes to incentives, new freedoms, such as walking to the store on their own or deciding for themselves when they do their homework, are often the best motivators. You can even tie the job and incentive together—you should have little difficulty persuading children like these to take sole responsibility for their own laundry (on the condition that it still gets done, of course).

Recognize employees

BUSINESS TIP:

According to a recent survey of what gives people the most job satisfaction, recognition was at the top of the ratings. If you want to motivate your staff, make sure you recognize good work and comment on it. That doesn't simply mean giving them a pat on the back, however. If you want to get the best results from recognition, you need to do more.

Follow these guidelines for effective recognition.
▶ Make recognition specific.
▶ Talk about recognition.
▶ Make recognition public.
▶ Pass on recognition from others.

Children are deeply motivated by parental approval, and recognizing your children when they do well will encourage them to do well again. It is a carrot rather than a stick technique for getting good behavior from your children, and one that will build their confidence and self-esteem at the same time. Apply the business guidelines to the way you recognize your children, and motivate them as strongly as possible.

▶ Make recognition specific

BUSINESS TIP:

You need to do more than say, "Well done." Tell your staff exactly what you're recognizing them for. Show them that you really noticed. For example, you might say, "You all did a terrific job of pulling together that presentation so quickly," or

> "Well done for calming that customer down. He was fuming, and you handled him so well that he left smiling."

You can recognize your children for big things or small ones, and the more the better. You might say, "Well done for getting such terrific grades on your exams, especially in French and geography." But on a lesser point, you might say to your three-year-old, "Wow! You managed to fold your socks all by yourself? Well done!" or "You were really good this evening about going to bed without a fuss." (Okay, that's not likely to happen. But this is just a hypothetical example.)

Look for opportunities to recognize your children. It may seem insincere if you comment every five minutes for things that you both take for granted (such as your sixteen-year-old managing to dress himself. Mind you, getting around to putting his clothes on can be worthy of recognition in some sixteen-year-olds.). Find plenty of opportunities to recognize genuine achievements, however small. Match your response to the importance of the achievement. It isn't necessary to send a press release to the local paper just because your six-year-old remembered to brush her teeth at bedtime without being reminded. You can still tell her how impressed you are.

▶ Talk about recognition

BUSINESS TIP:

> Show that you are genuinely interested in the achievements that you are recognizing your team member for. "I still can't get over how impressed the customer was at the end of it. I could hardly take down his order fast enough. How on earth did you manage to get the PowerPoint material ready so fast?"

Your child will feel really proud of herself if you show real interest in her achievement. Talk about it. "You've managed to fold those socks really neatly, too, and you put them back in the right drawer." Another good idea is to ask her questions about it (it's amazing how much you can find to say about folding socks when you need to): "How could you tell that you had them both the right way round before you started folding them?" When it comes to the exam results, you could ask, "Which questions in the geography exam did you think you'd done best on?"

When you talk about the achievement you're describing, there is one important rule: Never put a sting in the tail. If you finish with a negative point ("Shame about the biology result, though"), you will undo all the good work that you've just done. Next time you recognize your child's achievement, he will just be waiting for the "but . . . " at the end. Don't even mention that one of the folded socks in the pair is green and the other one has Thomas the Tank Engine all over it. It doesn't matter. She managed to fold them, and that's what you're talking about. Save any training on how to identify a matching pair for another time.

▶ Make recognition public

BUSINESS TIP:

Tell other people how well someone did. Put it in the company newsletter if it's important enough. Mention that person at a meeting when your boss is there. Write to the managing director to draw attention to the excellent presentation given. Even when you're recognizing a minor achievement, there's often an opportunity to mention it to a colleague or raise it at a team meeting. "Hey, Pat, have you seen the stationery cupboard since Jim reorganized it? I can find everything now!"

Telling someone else how well your child has done will mean a great deal to him, especially if it's someone whose good opinion he values. When your partner gets home, say, "You'll never guess what Nick did this morning," and make sure you say it in front of Nick. Or, tell your child, "I think I'll phone Granny right now and tell her that you know how to fold your own socks. I bet she'll be impressed."

▶ Pass on recognition from others

BUSINESS TIP:

> *Always tell your team members if someone else comments about their performance to you. For example, "I'm told that you gave a very slick presentation yesterday. When Jenny Smith called to place her order afterwards, she commented on how impressed she was." Or, even a simple, "Fred was saying this morning how much easier it is to find things in that stationery cupboard since you sorted it out."*

Passing on recognition is not only recognition from the other person, but from you, too; you clearly took it on board and thought it worth passing on. You give double the satisfaction by handing on recognition in this way. It might be, "Your French teacher told me she wasn't surprised you did so well in the exam. You've been doing really well all term, I gather." Or, "Granny says that when you were over there this weekend, you matched up her gloves and folded them all by yourself. She appreciated your help."

FIVE

Management Tips

Managing children can be much like managing your team at work. Sure, children can be difficult, uncompromising, and manipulative, but then so can staff on occasion. Both need to be motivated in order to get them to do what you want. They also need to be kept in check, sometimes even disciplined, when they step out of line.

Of course, you need to work doubly hard to manage your children well because, as mentioned previously, they have one great hold over you that your staff lack—you can't fire them. Imagine being saddled with the same team at work for eighteen years, with no chance of them retiring, getting promoted, moving on, or even, if their performance is truly dreadful, being given a pink slip. You'd have to work diligently at your management skills to make sure that you all worked well and productively without throttling each other for all that time. Well, now's your chance to practice . . . on your children.

Children are all different, just as grown-ups are, and you'll have different problems with each of them if you have more than one. Some are easy to handle, some whine dreadfully or sulk, and others like to bend the rules. Later in this chapter I will give you a surefire guide on managing some of the classic behaviors you're most likely to come across in your children. You'll probably recognize most of them from staff you've worked with, too.

Give feedback

BUSINESS TIP:

> Sometimes certain team members can be particularly difficult to work with. Maybe a person is constantly negative or critical or lazy or just too jolly and loud. The trick is to keep from bottling the thing up or, on the other hand, to avoid snapping at the person or flying off the handle. Feedback is a way to handle these difficult team members.

Follow these suggestions to give feedback effectively.
▶ Plan what you want to say in advance.
▶ Find a quiet, unhurried opportunity to talk in private.
▶ Focus on how you feel, not on what the person does.
▶ Listen to the other person's side of the story.
▶ Be positive about future behavior.
▶ Suggest a solution.
▶ Be prepared to compromise.

Feedback also works at home with the children. Whether it seems like they're forever leaving the milk out of the fridge, or always whining on long car journeys, or never hanging the towels back on the rail after their baths, you can resolve the whole thing without having to argue about it. Now, doesn't that sound refreshing?

▶ Plan what you want to say in advance
BUSINESS TIP:

> The core of feedback, that which makes it a successful technique, is that it entails phrasing what you say carefully so as not to make the other person feel defensive. To be sure of getting this right, you need to decide ahead of time what you're going to say. The four key rules are to refrain from exaggeration, avoid judgements, avoid labels, and be ready to cite specific instances.

Feedback is the only approach that gives you a chance to tackle thorny topics with your child without the encounter ending in tears (quite possibly your own). The system is designed to focus on the behavior and not the child, so that any criticism seems indirect. The first step in the process is to outline the problem as you see it. You do this by being fair and observing the first three rules above: no exaggerations, judgements, or labels.

Very few people accept negative criticism readily, and I suspect your child is no exception. For criticism to be positive, you have to be fair and objective from the start, and avoid any negative remarks. You will inevitably anger and demoralize your child if you imply that there is a constant problem when, in fact, it is only occasional. If you say, "You never help with anything," your child, who probably does help from time to time, will wonder why she bothers at all if you don't notice the good behavior. Remarks such as, "You're always complaining" (although in the case of a few people, children included, this is no exaggeration) or "You never think of anyone but yourself" are not helpful and are usually exaggerations.

Avoiding judgements means addressing the problem from a neutral perspective, without implying any moral standard to it. There is no need to tell your child that she is useless at this, or selfish about that. Simply state what she does without adding any moral or subjective comments. Of course, your child may well be selfish about not helping, but the aim of the exercise is to solve the problem, not to vent your feelings. Keep your judgements to yourself, and just say, "You don't often help me get meals ready or clear up afterwards." Telling her she is selfish may make you feel better, but is it really going to encourage her to be more helpful?

The third rule is to avoid labels. If you label a child in a negative way, he starts to feel that he is selfish or naughty or whatever label it is that you've applied to him. He can't change his nature, so he might as well give up. If he feels the label is unfair or inaccurate, he will equally wonder what is the point of trying to be helpful if you're just going to perceive him as being useless anyway. Avoid saying, "You're a selfish boy," or "You're stupid," or "You never think of anyone but yourself." You need

"I think Mom's feeling defensive."

to approach him with the attitude that he is not a selfish child, he is a good child who has done a selfish thing. Far better to put him in a positive light and say, "It's not like you at all. You're usually so helpful."

Positive labels are obviously far better for building children's self-esteem and confidence and giving them something to live up to. By all means, tell a child he is friendly, clever, helpful, or thoughtful, but with two provisos: only use accurate positive labels and describe what he did that earned him such recognition. For example, "You are such a friendly boy. You played with that new boy down the road and showed him where to find the best leeches." Children know when a compliment is untrue. They are undermined if you label them as clever, but their school grades never live up to your expectations. Or, if you label them as helpful when they're not, they'll see no reason to improve. Feel free, however, to use accurate labels that are positive and tell your child what he did that impressed you.

Finally, be ready with concrete examples. Your child is likely to say, "When have I been whiny about going shopping?" or "But I helped you set the table yesterday. When am I not helpful?" You'd better have answers ready to these questions, or the conversation could get very sticky. Your child is hardly going to settle for "Oh, I can't remember exactly. But I'm sure you're whiny quite often." If you can't come up with any examples beforehand, are you even sure that your criticism is fair?

▶ Find a quiet, unhurried opportunity to talk in private

BUSINESS TIP:

If you're going to offer criticism to a person about her job performance, however constructively, you need to do it in as relaxing an atmosphere as possible to help to keep the encounter pleasant. Never embarrass someone by giving feedback in front of other people. And make sure the meeting is no longer than necessary to cover the issue.

If your child is just about to rush outside to ride his bike before that black rain cloud bursts, it's not a good time to try to get his undivided attention for a few minutes. Equally, you should not attempt to give feedback when he is engrossed in a television program, doing his homework (you should be so lucky), having a group of friends over, or is in the middle of an argument with you about how to stack the dishwasher properly.

Wait until you can catch your child on his own (in the case of some teenagers, you may have to wait several weeks for this) and not rushing off to do something. Sit down, in order to avoid the impression that you are about to disappear somewhere, and have a quiet chat with him.

It's not a good idea to try to give feedback while your child is exhibiting the problem behavior because it's much harder for both of you to remain calm and objective. In other words, when he says, "But I hate doing the shopping. Why do I always have to come with you?" this is not the moment to reply, "That reminds me, I wanted to talk to you about your whining."

▶ Focus on how you feel, not on what the person does

BUSINESS TIP:

> *Always start your sentences with "I feel . . . " You might say, "I feel frustrated when I want to look at the big picture and you want to discuss details." Explain why you feel this way, "I feel my time is being wasted on matters you are capable enough to deal with on your own." Saying accusingly, "You do this," or "You make me feel . . . " will put the person on the defensive.*

Children are not known for being humble when criticized, and leveling accusations at them will generate at least as strong a reaction as it does with people at work. If you say to your child, "You ruin my evenings by playing loud music when I'm trying to relax," you can't expect her to say, "I'm so sorry. I never thought of that. How inconsiderate of me; it must be awful for you. I'll never put my CDs on after half past seven in the future." Actually, there is a possibility she will say that, but only with a strong note of sarcasm in her voice.

Start with the words, "I feel" and see if you can't phrase the same thing in a less confrontational way. How about: "I feel frustrated when you play your music loudly in the evenings. It's my first chance to wind down after a long day, and I can't relax to loud music." There. That doesn't warrant an outburst in response; it's a perfectly balanced, reasonable comment, with no exaggeration, judgements, or labels, and expressed from your own perspective. And you also explained the problem.

Here's another example: "I feel taken for granted when I've prepared a meal for you and you don't offer to help clear up afterwards. It takes quite a lot of time and energy, and a few minutes' input from you would be a big help." Or, maybe: "I feel angry and worried when you go out without telling me. I'm responsible for you and concerned for your safety, and I feel helpless when I don't know where you are."

Always express the problem from your own perspective, and explain briefly why you see it as a problem.

▶ Listen to the other person's side of the story

BUSINESS TIP:

Once you've expressed your point of view, give the other person a chance to respond. Otherwise, she will become frustrated quickly, and that will waste all the good work you've done so far.

Few things irritate children more than not being listened to. It's a child thing. Children are very conscious that their view often counts for less than anyone else's—or seems to. The fastest way to wind up a child is to ignore, or appear to ignore, his feelings. If you do this, you've blown your delicate, non-confrontational approach and are back into full-scale warfare.

Once you've outlined the issue, give your child a chance to reply straight away. You'll get another chance to respond as soon as she has finished. For the time being, simply listen without interrupting, and make it obvious. Even if she has a pathetic argument ("I have to play my music loudly or I can't hear it well enough"), she still has a right to express her feeble attempt to wriggle out of the situation.

She might have a really good point to make. "I didn't realize you wanted help at mealtimes. You've never asked for it." If this is true, you can probably resolve things easily if you accept her point of view. Instead of retorting, "Well, I'm asking now!" or "I shouldn't have to ask!" you'll get a better result if you say, "That's a fair point, actually. How about I ask you now. Do you think you could help me out once a day at mealtimes?" (Obviously, you shouldn't have to ask, but, equally obviously, with children you always do have to ask. It's just one of those things.)

▶ Be positive about future behavior

BUSINESS TIP:

Let the team member know that you believe she can behave cooperatively. Show that you're being fair and friendly about the issue by pointing out when she has been cooperative. "I know you can be positive rather than negative. You were really positive despite the problems we had over meeting the quota last month."

This is another angle on not labeling, and a more positive one, too. If you're telling your child, however tactfully you put it, that she is a whiner, there is danger that she will conform to that image. Remind her that she is usually cooperative. Give her a specific example: "You were great fun to be out with when we went shopping at the beginning of last week, so I know you can be cooperative."

▶ Suggest a solution

BUSINESS TIP:

There's no point in complaining about something if you can't think of a better way of doing it. When it comes to finding a solution, you need to be realistic. The most important thing to

> remember is that you can't change someone's personality, you can only change behavior.

If you try to turn your messy child into a tidy one, you will both become demoralized and frustrated when it doesn't happen. What you can do, however, is turn her into a messy child who hangs up the bathroom towels when she has finished using them, instead of leaving them on the floor. Tackle individual behaviors, not the whole personality. By the way, the bathroom towels won't be folded neatly and carefully over the towel rail—they'll still be a mess. But at least the mess will be on the rail instead of on the floor.

Before you begin feedback, you need to have thought through a reasonable, workable solution that takes into account your child's point of view as well as your own, and doesn't attempt to change her natural personality. Your child might volunteer a different solution (if the problem is that she is always negative, she will probably pick holes in your solution anyway), but you should have one to offer. Perhaps you could agree on a schedule for helping with meals, or maybe it could become your child's job to set the table for each meal.

Your small child who doesn't like shopping may need an incentive to stop whining. To be frank, any child who doesn't like supermarket shopping clearly has a natural, sensible, healthy approach to life. Nevertheless, you probably don't enjoy it any more than he does, and being accompanied round the store by a small, whining object doubtless does nothing to improve the experience for you. Maybe you could suggest that if he doesn't complain (at least, not beyond the necessary token objection that any self-respecting child has to raise), you'll buy him a small treat at the end of the shopping trip. You'll have to stick to this firmly, of course. If you give in and buy him a bar of chocolate or a toy when he has been whiny, you'll have wasted all this effort, and you'll be out of pocket buying treats, too.

▶ Be prepared to compromise

BUSINESS TIP:

> Listen to the team member's response to your solution, and be ready to compromise if necessary. She may have a valid point, too, and it's only fair that you should meet in the middle by coming up with a solution that suits you both.

Be ready to compromise with your child. She might be prepared to turn down her loud music, but not by as much as you'd like. Or, perhaps she doesn't mind turning it off for an hour each evening if she can have it at full volume the rest of the time. You may well find yourself in a negotiation at this point, but you know all about how to do that now, so you'll be fine.

Feedback is the best way to sort out minor criticisms and gripes with your child without it leading to rows and unpleasantness. As your children get older, you can teach them how to do it consciously so that they can use feedback to minimize arguments with each other. And if, heaven forbid, they ever have a criticism of you, they can even use feedback to address that, too.

Handle mistakes

BUSINESS TIP:

> The vast majority of accidents, especially in a well-motivated team, are genuine mistakes. If the person who has made the mistake truly regrets it, there is no advantage to be gained by giving him a hard time about it. You will simply build up resentment. Avoid criticizing people for making genuine mistakes. Make sure they understand how it happened and have learned from it. Thank them for being honest enough to own up to it. That way, they will be happy (less reluctant, anyway) to tell you next time they make a mistake.

Have you ever been angry about being criticized for a mistake that you never saw coming, and were sorry it happened? You probably felt really resentful when someone pointed it out. The person telling you off apparently didn't think you were capable of feeling contrite without his reproof. That doesn't say much for his opinion of you. And when it's not even true—you were already feeling sorry—it's just demoralizing.

If you want to show your child that you respect her, one of the best ways is to accept her apology for a mistake without criticizing her. Obviously, this doesn't apply to repeated mistakes that she should have learned to avoid by now, such as yet another coffee ring on your polished antique table. This may stray into the realm of the discipline interview, which we'll look at next.

You will be able to keep the number of discipline interviews down if you prevent mistakes from recurring. When your child makes an avoidable mistake, it's not enough simply to smile indulgently and say, "There, there. It wasn't your fault." You need to discuss it without allocating blame.

The first thing to say is, "That's okay. I know you didn't mean that to happen." Then follow it up by checking that she now understands the problem: "Do you understand now why putting my favorite wool sweater through the wash made it shrink?" Make sure she understands, and then ask, "How will you make sure it doesn't happen again?" (other than by throwing away the sweater, which is now ruined for good). Be sure that she is aware of what she needs to do to avoid a similar mistake in the future. You could settle for, "I'll never, ever try to do your washing for you again," but ideally she'll understand that she mustn't put anything woollen through the washing machine, and that if she is in doubt she should ask first. Children's mistakes represent your golden opportunity to do some teaching.

Discipline

BUSINESS TIP:

No manager likes to discipline staff, but it will always be easier and more effective if you approach the whole thing in a calm, matter-of-fact, pragmatic manner. Out-of-control emotions get in the way of successful disciplining. While you have

"If you want to go to the lake, you'll have to clear it with Human Resources."

> no control over the other person's emotions, you can certainly keep on top of your own.

The first step, before you discipline anyone, is to check your facts. There are two basic areas to check:
- The person's performance,
- The standard for the job.

▶ The person's performance

BUSINESS TIP:

> It's humiliating for you, and unpleasant for the other person, if you try to discipline him for something he hasn't done. When you accuse your employee of having been late three times last week, only to discover that he had cleared it with his supervisor, you're going to feel pretty silly, and he will feel unfairly criticized.

If you accuse your child of stealing money from your wallet, and she denies it, you'll be at an instant stalemate unless you've checked what actually happened. You need to establish what happened, and be able to prove it if there's any chance of denial. Do this in advance so that you are confident of your facts. What's more, your child will soon learn that there's no point denying these things because you're bound to have evidence. You always do.

▶ The standard for the job

BUSINESS TIP:

> You also need to be clear about what your employee thinks is expected of him. If you've never made it clear what time he was supposed to arrive, you can't very well tell him he's late just because you've decided that he should be in by half past nine. Unless the other person knew that what he was doing was wrong or not up to standard, you shouldn't be disciplining him at all.

It's possible your child thought that it was okay to take money from your wallet so long as it was for a legitimate reason. Perhaps it was her school lunch money for the week, or maybe you told her a couple of weeks ago that you'd pay for her to go swimming. Having got your facts straight on these two areas, the child's performance and the standard expected, the purpose of disciplining is simple. You need to close the gap between the two. If her performance hasn't reached the standard you expect, you need to do three things in your discipline interview.

- Get her agreement that there is a gap. ("Yes, I know. I'm not allowed to take money from your wallet without permission.")
- Establish why there is a gap. ("I was really hungry and I could not find anything in the house I wanted, so I went down to the corner store to get some pizza and a soda pop.")
- Find a way to close the gap. ("All right. I'll pay you back out of my allowance next week and I won't do it again.")

One of the key rules about disciplining someone for a persistent problem is to catch it early. If your child takes money from your wallet once, you might overlook it. As soon as it happens again, deal with it. Don't wait until it has happened four or five times. There are two reasons for this.

First, it makes the discipline interview far easier. You're only dealing with a very minor problem at this stage, so there's no need for anyone to get heated or upset. You're simply tweaking her performance slightly, not completely overhauling it. It's far easier to get your child to pay back the money she borrowed from you when it's only five dollars, than to wait until she has built up a debt of five hundred dollars.

Second, the very fact that you haven't said anything will have implied that you were happy with the way she was performing. If she has been regularly taking small amounts of money and you have never noticed or said anything, she has probably concluded by now that it was perfectly acceptable, or that you were terribly easy to fool.

Conduct effective interviews

Several guidelines help in conducting a discipline interview in a calm manner that will lead to the behavior you are looking for.

BUSINESS TIP:

> We've already seen that you need to be relaxed and calm to conduct the interview. For example, if you're fuming about the fact that your employee has made a crucial decision without consulting you, wait until you've calmed down before you talk to him about it. If he becomes emotional, be sympathetic, but don't allow it to put you off or change your standards.

Follow these five rules of engagement.
- Get the person to talk.
- Stick to the facts.
- Focus on the problem, not the person.
- Maintain confidentiality.
- Be consistent.

▶ Get the person to talk

BUSINESS TIP:

> You need to establish the reasons for the gap between the standard for the job and the employee's actual performance. If you want your employee's cooperation, this information is far better coming from him. Keep your opinion to yourself for the moment; ask him why he hasn't met the agreed standard. Encourage him to open up and talk about it by asking him open-ended questions, such as, "What was the reason that you made this decision without discussing it with me first?"

Get your child to talk about what happened rather than sulk silently. Ask him questions beginning "Why . . . ?", "How . . . ?", "In what way . . . ?" and so on. For example, "How come you left the bathroom for half an hour after you'd turned the bathtub faucet full on?"

▶ Stick to the facts
BUSINESS TIP:

> A team member may well try to wriggle out of the spot or get defensive by coming up with all sorts of excuses for his behavior. You can get round this simply by coming back to the facts. "But you did make the decision yourself even though I was around to ask."

Any self-respecting child is going to try to come up with an excuse. "I just went to answer the phone," or "I fell asleep," or "I thought I'd forgotten to put the plug in."

Just keep bringing him back to the facts, gently but firmly. "Nevertheless, the living room was flooded and the computer reacted by blowing up. This was because you left the bathtub faucet running for half an hour."

▶ Focus on the problem, not the person
BUSINESS TIP:

> If you want to keep the mood relaxed and mature, focus on the employee's action, not his personality. Avoid comments such as "You're arrogant," or "Your problem is that you think you can do everything yourself." That is not the problem. The problem is that a decision was taken without reference to you when you should have been asked to approve it.

Children are great at saying, "Well, I was only . . . " or "I just thought. . . ." Resist the urge to say, "No, you didn't, you never think. That's your problem." This breaks all the rules we've established already (refrain from exaggeration, avoid labels, and several others, including your own promise to yourself that you'd never sound like your mother once you had children). More to the point, criticizing doesn't work. Children feel defensive and become understandably emotional, which gets in the way of a successful discipline interview.

Never mind telling them that they're always absentminded, or thoughtless, or in a dream. Maybe they are. But they can't change the way they are, so there's no point in trying to make them (anyway, it's what you love them for, isn't it? Remind yourself of that while you're cleaning up the flood downstairs and earning the money to get the computer fixed). Just concentrate on the problem, which is that the house was flooded because the bathtub faucet was left on, not that you have an irresponsible child.

▶ Maintain confidentiality

BUSINESS TIP:

> *Keep to yourself any details of what was said at a discipline interview. You'll never get anyone to talk freely in such an interview again if you breach confidentiality, and you'll upset the person deeply. Even if the discipline resulted from a complaint by someone else, that person needs to know only that the matter has been dealt with. Your employee, on the other hand, can say what he likes to anyone about it.*

It's important for your child to feel that once the problem is resolved and the interview is over, the matter is forgotten (assuming that necessary lessons have been learned, such as turning the faucet off before leaving the room). The child isn't left with a sinking feeling or a sense that there is trouble in the air. One of the most important ways to do this is to keep the matter confidential once it's sorted out.

Keep quiet about what happened and what was said. If your child's best friend's mother says to him, "I hear you flooded the house the other day. And you claimed you'd fallen asleep!" he will think twice before he opens up to you about anything else.

Yes, I know that it's impossible not to tell close family members when your four-year-old cutely explains that she only took the money from your wallet "to leave it out for Santa Claus, because nobody pays him for working so hard." But if there's any chance that your child will mind if you pass on what she has said or what action she has agreed to take, at least restrict yourself to telling people who will keep it to themselves. If you possibly can, don't even tell them.

▶ Be consistent

BUSINESS TIP:

> Make sure that you apply the same rules to everyone. If you come down hard on John for being late twice when you gave Phil only a mild telling-off for being late half a dozen times, you'll build up resentment very quickly, along with accusations of favoritism.

If you have more than one child, you need to make sure that you discipline and punish them all equally for comparable offences. This means remembering what punishments you have meted out in the past, because you know perfectly well that your children will remember them with stunning accuracy. "But you made him go to bed half an hour early for a week, and now you're making me go to bed an hour early for four nights. You're punishing me for half an hour more than him!" You could try arguing that it's all down to inflation, but you'd be better off getting it right in the first place. Keep a notebook or a diary if you need to.

Once you've agreed on the action that you and your child are both going to take to close the gap between standards and performance, you need to make sure it happens. This includes making it clear what will happen if the problem recurs. Speculation is out of the question. Tell your child, "If it happens again, I will have to run the bath water for you," or "You'll be banned from using the bathtub for a month" (although I don't recommend this particular one unless you also have a shower). Make sure that the child knows exactly where he stands, and there's much less chance that he will need disciplining again. Well, at least not for that particular offence.

Deal with people who create problems

We like to think that our children will grow up to be sensible, rational adults. But experience shows us that many of the grown-ups we know haven't managed it. Many of our colleagues, bosses, or staff members exhibit traits that we fondly hope our children will have outgrown long before they are released into the community.

However, the good news is that if you know how to cope with people who manipulate, sulk, whine, and the like at work, you can also handle them at home. If your son blames his big sister for everything, or your daughter goes into deep sulks, you can apply the same techniques to them as you do to a team member who always passes the buck, or a colleague who sulks at the slightest excuse.

The thing to remember about these people, of whatever generation, is that you cannot change their innate personalities, and you shouldn't try. Someone who daydreams will always do so. Your task is to find a way to cope with the daydreaming, or put it on hold when things need to be given fuller concentration. Here are suggestions for dealing with people who:

▶ Never listen,
▶ Daydream,
▶ Manipulate others or the situation,
▶ Pass the buck,
▶ Whine,
▶ Sulk,
▶ Act like prima donnas.

▶ People who never listen

BUSINESS TIP:

> The problem with people who do not listen is that they often fail to do things, or they do them wrong, and then claim that you never asked them to do the job, or that you didn't mention that they'd have to check with the accounting department first. The solution is to get them to repeat instructions back to you. If you think they're repeating them in a parroting fashion, without actually taking them in, ask open questions about the task: "How do you think we should deal with visual aids for the presentation?" "How long do you think it will take the crew to complete this job?"

"What are you staring at? This is just a temp job."

How often have you heard your child excuse herself for not doing something by saying, "You never asked me to!" Some children genuinely believe this is true; they're not trying to be naughty. They really didn't hear you. If you need them to hear an instruction or a piece of information ("Great Auntie Marjorie's coming to dinner, so watch your language"), follow it by saying, "I want to be sure I've made this clear. Could you repeat it back to me?"

If they reply in a fashion that gives you the least suspicion that they haven't actually heard you, or have not understood you, ask them an open-ended question, "What words do you particularly need to avoid when Great Auntie Marjorie is here?"

▶ People who daydream

BUSINESS TIP:

> *People who daydream tend to get distracted in the middle of tasks, and they make mistakes or become sidetracked. Anything they find boring is especially likely to send them off into their dream world. Keep them stimulated and interested, and give them tasks to do with other people. A colleague can help keep them wide awake and focused on the job.*

Your child is always going to daydream if she's bored. And often, it's a good quality. She probably whines less because she can withdraw into a world that is always interesting, and she probably has a wonderful imagination. However, imagination won't get the bedroom tidied or the homework finished.

Forget about trying to give your daydreamer boring, monotonous jobs to do unless she can either dream as she does them (like drying the dishes), or you don't mind how many weeks elapse before the task is complete. You'll get better results if you give her interesting jobs to do that actively engage her mind.

If boring tasks need doing (and let's face it, the chores at the top of the list always seem boring), do them together so that you can keep her alert. Or, if you have more than one child, get them to share two tasks between them, rather than doing one each. This may be the greater of the two evils if they're inclined to fight, but for some siblings it works very well.

▶ People who manipulate others or the situation

BUSINESS TIP:

> *The key to understanding people who manipulate is to recognize that they always have a hidden motive. They will never give you enough evidence that you can use to prove they're manipulating, so an open challenge can be denied. But you can work out why they're doing it if you're clever, and then tackle the root cause. If Jenny is trying to make Dave look bad, maybe it's because she wants the promotion when Phil leaves, and she's worried you'll promote Dave instead. Simply talk to her and say, "I get the feeling that you might be interested in Phil's job when it comes up. Is that right?" This gives her the chance to be open rather than underhanded with you. She'll go for it, because it gives her a better chance of getting what she wants.*

You know that it was Harriet who planted your wallet in Max's bed to get him into trouble. But you can't prove it. It's all right, you don't need to. Just work out why Harriet wants to get Max into trouble. Is she jealous of him? Is she paying him back for getting her into trouble yesterday? Whatever the reason, sit Harriet down and talk to her about it. If you reckon she's trying to pay Max back, say, "I sense that you're still angry with Max for filling your boots with yogurt yesterday. Am I right?"

Perhaps Harriet feels that Max wasn't sufficiently punished, or that everyone thinks his practical jokes are funny, and she doesn't get enough sympathy. You can't backdate Max's punishment, but you could offer to talk to him again, or assure Harriet that any future yogurt incidents will incur more serious punishments (and tell Max, too). Whatever you agree to, you have removed the need for any manipulative behavior. Oh, and the wallet in the bed never needs to be mentioned at all.

▶ People who pass the buck

BUSINESS TIP:

> Those who pass the buck always believe that bad things happen because someone else is at fault. "Sorry I didn't get the filing on your desk cleared by Monday, but Kieran suddenly dumped a load of work on my desk on Thursday." You have to make it absolutely clear to these people exactly what needs to be done, and make it clear that if there's a problem you must be told straight away. If someone comes to you on Thursday complaining that the job won't be done on time, just use the stuck-record technique, "The extra work from Kieran obviously makes it harder, and I still need all the filing cleared by Monday." If he continues to protest, ask him, "What are you going to do about Kieran's work to make sure my filing is still cleared by Monday?"

The child who blames school, a brother or sister, a parent or a friend for every failure to deliver the goods needs to learn that it is her responsibility to cope with the problems that all these other people seem to throw at her. You need to make it clear that she still has to dry the dishes after dinner, or whatever the task is. Be specific about what you want. "I want all the dishes dried, and I want it done straight after the meal, not later in the evening."

If she says, "Sarah's coming over and she'll be here by half past seven, so I won't have time," simply reiterate the task. "I can see that's difficult, and you still need to dry the dishes straight after dinner." Keep persisting. Suppose the next excuse is, "Sarah's already bought tickets for a movie and it starts at 7:45, so I won't have time," just keep going. Make it clear that it is her responsibility to cope with these problems and still get the job done. Ask, "How are you going to arrange it so that the dishes still get done straight away?"

In this case, the ultimate sanction, of course, is that she will have to miss the movie. Once she learns that you won't back down, she will have to figure out how to cope with Sarah or whoever else it may be and fulfill her responsibilities, no matter what.

▶ People who whine

BUSINESS TIP:

> People who whine are generally a bit of a pain to have on your team. On the other hand, they often cause everyone else to keep quiet. The fact that they are guaranteed to moan means that everyone else feels they don't have to. The more you can involve them in what's going on, the less they will whine. If they helped to formulate a decision, they can't very well complain about it. The other specific technique you can use is to ask them before they start to whine if they need any help. If they say "yes," you can provide it. If they say "no," it's harder for them to complain later.

For many parents, the classic whiner is the one who complains about long car journeys (he usually starts whining before he's even into the car). Maybe you can involve him in the decision to make the journey. Ask him if he'd like to go on vacation to the ocean, instead of just booking it yourself without consulting him. Remind him about the long journey. When it comes to it, at least he'll realize he volunteered for it.

The day or morning before the journey, ask him if he needs anything to keep himself amused. Be prepared to supply magazines or games or packages of crackers if he asks (though perhaps you might draw the line at going out and buying him a laptop computer). Not only should this do the trick, but he'll feel you sympathize with his low boredom level on long journeys, rather than simply being irritated by it.

▶ People who sulk

BUSINESS TIP:

> Sulking is designed to make you feel guilty once you realize how deeply upset the person sulking is. If you are guilty, you should apologize, which is what the employee wants. Once you've apologized (sincerely and appropriately), she'll stop sulking. However, you may not feel guilty in the least. In this case, reassure yourself that the person sulking has really had a

> fair chance to have her say. Many of us sulk if we feel we're not being taken seriously, so make sure that this isn't the case (and if it is, hear her out). If you're clear on this score, too, don't capitulate. If you ever give in to someone sulking, letting her find out it works, she'll try it every time she's unhappy. Just ignore her and say, "We'll discuss it later." Don't make things worse by sulking or fuming back. Pretend everything's normal, and she'll give up when she finds that sulking doesn't work.

A sulky child can bring a heavy atmosphere over the whole household. On the other hand, the ones who don't sulk probably throw tantrums, which is arguably worse. At least, with sulkers you can get on with your life and ignore them.

Be a stickler for the rules. If you've said your child can't have a motorbike, he can't have a motorbike. Let him see that sulking isn't going to help one jot. And then behave as if he isn't sulking anyway. It's a slow business, but over the months and years you can train a child out of sulking this way (well, most of the time). If you give in to it, however, he will get worse. That's probably what your sulky colleague's parents did.

▶ People who act like prima donnas

BUSINESS TIP:

> Prima donna types never sulk—they throw tantrums instead. "I can't believe you let someone else handle that contract! After all the work I'd put into it! For crying out loud!" Like those who sulk, they do it because it works. Resist. Take the wind right out of their sails by leaving the room. "I'm just going to get myself a cup of coffee. I'll talk to you about this later." You should also (if you are trapped in the room with them) refuse to get heated and emotional in response. Simply be cool, rational, and objective.

At home, the standard approach with a junior prima donna type should be to ignore him completely. Behave as if he weren't there. It will drive him mad this time, but in the long term it will show him that his method doesn't work. Leave the room because without an audience, he's lost. If he follows you, you can either ignore him or send him to his room.

If you send him to his room, however, don't show any sign of being emotional yourself (because that's what he wants, to know he's getting to you). Just smile and say, "Off you go to your room. You're being a bit too noisy to stay down here. You can come down when you're calm, and if you want me to, I'll talk to you again about why you can't have a motorbike. See you in a bit. Bye."

Give him all the time he wants to talk, discuss, and reason when he's calm, but refuse to talk when he becomes emotional. It won't take him long to realize which behavior is in his best interest.

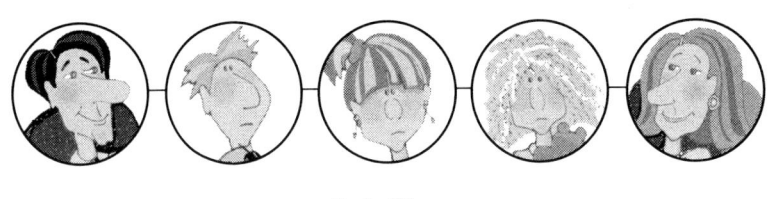

SIX

Teamwork Tips

The most frustrating parts of being a parent, if you have more than one child, are the constant arguments and endless sniping and tale-telling that can go on between children. It's a shame because you want them all to be friends. And the older they get, the more you want them to look out for each other and be supportive when things are tough. If you think about it, brothers and sisters probably know each other for longer than they know anyone else in their lives. Even when you're not there for them any more, you'd like to know that they will be there for each other.

That's why teamwork skills are so useful in bringing up a family. Not only do they minimize the arguments (I'm afraid I'd be lying if I claimed that they remove them altogether), but they also help bond your children into a strong and supportive unit. The aim is to have a family that functions as an effective team, with the children as a kind of sub-team within it.

There are several management techniques that have a long track record of effectiveness in helping to pull together a group of people into a team, even when the department includes people of many ages and from a wide range of backgrounds. These techniques should be a piece of cake with your kids, who are from the same background and are relatively close in age. You simply have to know how to motivate your children to care about the team unit, the family, so that they are not focused solely on themselves.

"Read me again the one about the three pigs and the wolf who tried to downsize them."

It's also worth bearing in mind another team-building principle: nothing unites people better than a common enemy. You may have noticed how a team at work that is so rife with friction that it hardly merits the title "team" will suddenly pull together in the face of a strong competitor who is likely to steal a contract from them, or a board that might decide to base them twenty miles away at a different branch office.

With your children, the most promising common enemy is you. This is not to say that you should go out of your way to behave like an enemy, but every so often your children will cast you that way because you said "no" to the new bike, or you shouted at them over dinner when they hadn't done anything wrong—they simply wanted to dunk their apple pie in the leftover gravy. As a result, they will moan and groan to each other about you.

Neither encourage nor discourage this. Their negative attitude will soon blow over, and in the meantime, they are building stronger ties with each other as they agree about how cruel and inhuman you are, in a way they have never agreed about anything else, such as which television channel to watch, or where to go for an outing. Shared bedrooms are a great way to encourage your children to complain about you together, also, along with sitting them next to each other in the back seat of the car (where they can whisper irritatingly just out of your earshot) or simply leaving them alone in a room together after you've refused a request or got angry with one of them.

The good news is that there are plenty of principles you can apply to family life to encourage your children to feel like part of a team, one that they want to belong to. Here are the key guidelines for building a great team at home.

Encourage mutual support

BUSINESS TIP:

If one member of your team needs help or advice, you don't always have to be the one to provide it. Suggest he ask a fellow team member, or ask someone else yourself to help him. This encourages the team to form good working relationships among themselves that don't have to incorporate you every

> *time. Equally, if one member of the team has a really urgent task to complete, get all available hands on deck to get it done.*

If one of your children needs help with her math homework, why not have her ask her older brother or sister to help instead of helping her yourself? It will make the older child feel important, and will enable the pair of them work together. Not to mention that it will leave you more time to get on with other things. It never hurts to get your children to help each other, whether it's washing each other's backs in the bath or learning to put on make-up.

However, if you want to help construct solid, equal relationships in the family, even the youngest child has to be able to give support as well as receive it. This child can certainly help out with chores (although he may not see it that way), and he may well be able to provide information that the others want: "Why not go and ask Jamie about that—he's the expert on leeches."

If you're looking for opportunities to encourage support between your kids, you should find that the youngest children develop particular skills quite early on. A six-year-old may have a talent for setting the timer on the video, and can be asked to do it for an older brother or sister. Or, he may know more than anyone else in the family about dinosaurs or trains. Don't miss a chance to refer an older sibling to a younger one for information, rather than supplying it yourself.

When one of your children has an urgent or difficult job to do, call everyone together who is free to help. If you make this fun, they will want to join in. Maybe your teenager is packing to go on a school trip and is running late. You can get everyone running round the house finding spare socks and tracking down a toiletries bag. Or, perhaps your ten-year-old is having trouble assembling her new go-cart and needs a hand. There are also family crises to involve everyone in, such as bailing out the basement when it floods after a heavy storm. If you enjoy dealing with the crisis, instead of panicking or barking orders, your children will enjoy it, too. And they'll learn that things go far more smoothly when they all pull together.

You can't call all hands on deck five times a day, or everyone will get fed up with the workload, but every few weeks it's a great team activity.

Give each person responsibility

BUSINESS TIP:

> You can encourage mutual respect among your team members by giving everyone some responsibility. It will help them to realize that people are in charge of tasks, not people. Having put someone in charge of a project, you must back her up publicly, and do things her way along with everyone else. If there are any problems, you should sort them out together behind closed doors.

This is a great technique to use with children; they really appreciate the responsibility. It may seem unfair to put one child in charge of something over the others, but it works so long as you bear in mind two important guidelines. Don't put children directly in charge of each other, only in charge of the task itself. And choose the responsibilities carefully to make sure they won't lead to major conflict.

For example, you could put one child in charge of the shopping list, making sure that if anyone uses up the last of something, it gets written down, and checking that there's always a shopping list pad with a pen next to it. This is a responsibility that involves everyone in the family, but doesn't put one child in charge of anyone else. Your child can, however, introduce a better system and ask everyone to follow it. The responsibilities you choose have to concern everyone, or they have no impact on your objective to foster team spirit. It's fine if one of your children is assigned to take the vegetable peelings out to the compost heap every day, but the task isn't going to impinge on their siblings, so it doesn't build team spirit.

If you want more suitable responsibilities, organizing practically anything and keeping it organized generally works well: sorting out the video cupboard, keeping the cupboard stocked with snack foods, or organizing the travel arrangements to and from school (best not to leave this to your five-year-old, mind you). Also, as we saw in the last chapter, give children tasks they are good at, and they'll enjoy them more.

If you're worried that your children will set unreasonable standards and then fight with the others when they don't stick to them ("You've got to color code every video as soon as you record it with one of these eight dots according to this code I've written down. If you don't, I'll wipe your video"), you can always stipulate that any new system should be cleared with you first.

Train the team collectively

BUSINESS TIP:

Group training sessions bring people together. Teaching staff to use computers and copiers and other office equipment is best done in groups, so that more experienced or mechanically minded team members can help others who are less skilled or daring. If they all need to know something, tell them all at once.

"Right, kids. This is how the new washing machine works." It's easier to tell everyone at the same time—you only have to go through it once. They all feel equally involved. What's more, they can giggle together when you get it wrong and flood the laundry room.

Recognize the team as a whole

BUSINESS TIP:

If the team works well together, recognize them collectively rather than recognizing each person individually. This reinforces the importance of the collective contribution everyone is making. Recognize everyone equally, whatever their contribution. A company celebration of a profit goal met, a department outing to celebrate mailing the new catalog on time (in spite of computer problems), or iced tea and cold watermelon on a hot day when everyone has been pleasant to hot and cranky customers can work wonders for team spirit.

If your children work well as a team, don't give them each some money or individual gifts. Buy ice cream all round, or take everyone out for a treat or a special meal. Think about redecorating a shared bedroom or playroom, or buying the popcorn maker they all want.

Because pleasure is a huge motivating factor, it's a good idea to create team activities that are fun, and then recognize achievement. For example, you could time how long it takes for you all to clear up after a meal. One stacks the dishwasher, one washes the pans, one clears and wipes the table, and so on. Every time you beat your previous record, everyone shares in the treat that follows (better check first that those pans really are clean).

Avoid areas of friction

BUSINESS TIP:

Avoid putting team members into close working relationships if you know that they're going to rub each other the wrong way. You can't force people to get along if they have personality conflicts. When you do have to ask them to work together, try to add a third person who can help to keep the peace.

If you've been following all the guidelines in this book, it's unlikely that you will have two children who really dislike each other. However, you probably will have two children who irritate each other in certain respects. Most parents do. When this happens, avoid putting them together for tasks that will obviously bring these problems to the fore.

Suppose one of your teenage children is careful and methodical, while another is slapdash and rushes everything. If you ask the two of them to redecorate their bedroom together, you're asking for trouble. Equally, it wouldn't be a good idea to get them to assemble the flat-packed wardrobe together. Either get a different child to do each job, or join in yourself and keep the peace by encouraging the methodical one to do the gloss work on the window trim while the slapdash one uses the roller on the walls. Meanwhile, you can try to put together the

114 • *Family Matters*

"You did such a great job that I'm treating you all to 401(k)s!"

wardrobe yourself and give them both a good laugh at your expense.

Discourage division within the team

BUSINESS TIP:

> *The unity of the team is crucial and more important than any petty disagreements within it. Discourage your team members from making complaints against each other or from running to you when a colleague has put one of their noses out of joint. Make it clear that you prefer them to sort out their differences by themselves.*

As soon as you take sides, however justified, you are splitting the team. This is clearly not something you want to do, so you need to avoid taking sides in the first place. Obviously, if one of your children hospitalizes the other, you're going to have to express a view. However, keep clear of everyday niggles of the "I was sitting there first" variety. You'll have to teach very young children to deal with these squabbles before you can take a back seat, but as they get older, they should be able to handle them alone.

The other thing to discourage firmly is tale-telling. It is guaranteed to divide the team if your children think they can get away with it. What a great way to get a brother or sister into trouble (to pay them back for swiping their seat). The only way to prevent this divisive behavior is to ensure that it doesn't work. When your ten-year-old daughter says, "Mark didn't do his homework last night, and then he told the teacher that he left it at home," your response depends on her motive for tale-telling. If she is trying to get her brother in trouble, your response should be, "Well, he shouldn't have done that, and likewise you shouldn't be tattling." Or, if she wants you to know she did her homework, you may respond, "I'm proud of you for getting your homework done, and you shouldn't be tattling on your brother."

To complete the effect, you now have to resist saying anything to Mark on the subject. This way, his younger sister has received a minor scolding and Mark has had none. It won't take long for it to sink in that telling tales gets you nowhere, and your children should learn that you value their loyalty to each other higher than any petty information they may pass on. They certainly won't snitch on each other if they are seeking your approval.

You have to intervene for health or safety's sake, for example, if one of your children tells you that her five-year-old sister is smoking ten cigarettes a day, but otherwise almost every time you're better off letting it pass. If the other child knows she's been snitched on, you may feel that you have to say something or you'll appear to condone the behavior. In that case, don't make her angry, or you'll encourage the tale teller, but simply say, "You got away with it this time. But don't let me catch you doing it."

Utilize each team member's strengths

BUSINESS TIP:

> *The better the team performs as a whole, the more motivated its members will be. They will see that they could not have achieved nearly so much alone, but that each member's contribution has been crucial. Give everyone the chance to shine for the benefit of the whole team. Give people tasks that put their strengths to productive use.*

We've touched on this before, but not in the context of building team spirit. However, it is important to allocate tasks in team activities according to each child's strengths. That way, at the end of the project, everyone will all see and value each other's input, and they'll realize that everyone else appreciates their contributions.

Maybe it's the last minute rush before you go off on a holiday. Get your methodical child to do the packing, while the hyperactive one cycles down to the store for a picnic to eat on the trip. Meanwhile, the organized one can gather up extra items that might have been forgotten to give to the sibling who is packing, such as first aid kit, sun block, flashlight, and so on. And you can have a rest—after you've sorted out the clean washing, tidied the house, checked that the windows are all locked, written the note for the milkman, taken the cat to the kennel, . . .

Just one thing to watch out for here: if you have two children with a similar strength, don't always give the jobs that require this quality to the same child. You may think Tom is pretty organized, but Sophie is the really organized one. However, if you always say, "Sophie, you can do this. You're always so good at organizing things," Tom is going to feel unappreciated. You may value the fact that he's the best problem-solver, but he will see only that you don't appreciate his organizational abilities. Make sure none of your children is harboring a secret feeling that he is being overlooked.

Communicate with your team

The way you communicate with your employees is a big part of helping them feel like a unit. If you treat them as a team, they will behave like a team. There are two key techniques for achieving this:

▶ Involve everyone in what's going on;
▶ Brief the team as a whole.

▶ Involve everyone in what's going on

BUSINESS TIP:

You can't expect your team to feel like part of a strong unit if they have no input into what that unit does or how it does it. Involve your team members in the decisions that will affect them. "Our workload is going to increase next month once the new system comes on line. How are we going to cope with it?" You can still make the final decision, but they will feel like part of the process.

One of the best ways to build up a strong family identity is to give your children a say in what goes on. Not only will they feel more motivated to cooperate, having been involved in the decision (even if it isn't the one they voted for), but they will also see that everyone else's opinion is important as well as their own. There are certainly times when you have to inform your children what's going on without their input ("Great Auntie Marjorie's coming to stay for two weeks"), but more often you can consult them before you make your final decision. "It's time to get rid of our worn-out car and get a new one. What do you all reckon we need in a family car? What features should it have?"

You'll find that when you give children this kind of opportunity, they live up to it admirably. They might want a Ferrari sports car or a gas-guzzling monster, but they know perfectly well that they're not going to get either one. They may have sensible suggestions to make about the amount of space it should have or a valid request for a sunroof. Even if they suggest nothing you haven't thought of already, they will still feel that they have a stake in the final decision. Who knows, they may even feel more inclined to keep the new car tidy.

Consult your children in a group. Family mealtimes are a good time for this. (In fact, family mealtimes in themselves are an important part of forming a team.) Unless you talk to them all at once, even though they will be individually motivated by being involved, you won't be doing anything for their feeling of team unity.

It's worth noting that current research shows that very few families have meals together nowadays, especially with the popularity of fast food and the increase in microwave use. However, shared mealtimes might be the only time families meet as a group, and they are enormously helpful in creating a feeling of team spirit. If you don't all eat together at the moment, consider introducing family mealtimes. If you can't all manage an evening meal together, perhaps you could all make breakfast at the same time. If you can't manage a family meal once a day, at least try to make it once a week.

▶ Brief the team as a whole

BUSINESS TIP:

> In order to engender a strong and positive group identity within the team, you need to talk to them as a team. Hold regular team briefings in which you pass on information that affects the group, and give them a chance to ask questions.

When anything important is happening in the family, call everyone together and brief them. "Okay, guys. We've got the builders in for the next two weeks, and here's what's going to be happening." Have a system, without making things incongruously formal, that they listen while you give the briefing, and then they ask questions afterwards. If they're not happy and want to whine about something, ask them to save it until after the briefing session. "I'm happy to talk to you about why you're not allowed to drive the mini-digger, but let's finish this first."

You don't have to save the team briefing for major events. If you really want to inculcate a feeling of unity, the best system of all is a drip-feed approach. Keep topping up the team feeling with weekly sessions, even if they're only five minutes long. Again, mealtimes are an easy time to hold these sessions, and Sunday evening is a good time to outline the week ahead. Of course, you should involve the children in fixing a suitable time for a regular briefing session. The older they get, the harder it is to assemble them all at once. Don't make this an unpleasant issue. Just get them to agree on a time that works for them all (of course, you may have to get them all together to agree to such a time). Maybe Monday morning breakfast will do. It's not as relaxed as Sunday, but if it works, go for it.

Deal with conflict and rivalry

Some conflict is inevitable. In fact, it can even be a good thing. Healthy competition can drive people to even greater results, whether it's the number of sales each one notches up in a month, or whether it's who can swim the length of the pool fastest or be the first to learn to ride a bicycle.

You already know that many of the conflicts arising between children aren't a good thing, however you look at them. If you follow all the guidelines in this book, you should find that your family life is as calm and pleasant as anyone's, and far better than most. Of course, there will still be the occasional problem. At home, as at work, there are three main causes of conflict between people.

- ▶ One person feels unfairly treated.
- ▶ One person feels excluded from the team.
- ▶ There is a personality clash.

Let's take a look at how to deal with each of these.

▶ One person feels unfairly treated

BUSINESS TIP:

You need to establish the facts, and if the person is indeed being unfairly treated, you should rectify this. However, even if you think things are fair, if someone feels she is being treated unfairly, then this will still lead to conflict. Get everyone involved together, and ask the person to express what she feels is unfair. Then you can oversee the discussion, making sure that no one gets personal or heated and helping everyone to reach a solution.

In team terms, we're talking about children who feel that their siblings are doing less work or have easier chores. If the gripe is only with you, it's not a team issue (and we'll have dealt with it in the previous chapter). But if Rosa reckons that Mike only has ten minutes of chores a day while she has twenty, she may be giving Mike a hard time for not taking over some of hers.

If you're a team, you have to resolve these problems as a team and not individually. You need Mike there, even if Rosa is being unrealistic. Maybe she just works slowly, and if they swapped chores, she'd still have twenty minutes' worth to Mike's ten. But with Mike there, too, the conflict can be discussed openly. Bear in mind that there are numerous reasons why people can feel that things are unfair. Maybe Rosa doesn't care how long the chores take, but she feels her tasks are less important or less interesting.

If Mike can see that she has a point, he is much more likely to cooperate in an atmosphere of open, friendly discussion. No one's blaming him or giving him a hard time, but he knows from experience that if he trades chores until Rosa is happy, he'll get plenty of recognition. And if he insists that her chores are no different from his, he won't mind changing, will he?

▶ One person feels excluded from the team

BUSINESS TIP:

If you want your team to pull together, you need to give them a sense of being a team. Once they learn that being part of a cooperative team is more pleasant than not, they will quickly learn to incorporate everyone into the team. You can help by treating everyone with equal importance, even though they may not have equal seniority. If you show that you listen to everyone's view equally and give everyone responsibilities that suit their skills, they will all learn to treat each other in the same way.

This problem arises most commonly when you have three children. Two play together, and the third is excluded because he's "too little" or she's "only a girl." Of course, you can't make your children play with each other all of the time. It's good for them to spend time alone or with friends outside of the family. But if the exclusion is handled unkindly ("Shove off! We don't want you around"), you'll have an unpleasant conflict to deal with.

If you've been following the rules earlier in this chapter, you should find that this arises much less often. Once your children feel like a team, they will be much more inclined to do things together. And if they don't want to, they'll say so nicely.

You can help things along by setting an example. If you allow the children to join in with you in fixing the car, decorating the spare bedroom, building the fence, and so on, they are more likely to allow each other to join in with them. If you show by example that everyone is capable of handling responsibility and can be trusted to behave sensibly, again you'll find

"No, Mindy, listen and wait your turn. Let Becky finish her Nobel Prize acceptance speech."

that your children follow suit with each other. Yes, you'll still get the occasional complaint of, "He won't let me play with his Transformers!" but you'll encounter far fewer conflicts arising from a sense of exclusion.

▸ There is a personality clash

BUSINESS TIP:

Bring the two people involved together, and get them to talk to each other directly, using feedback techniques. Point out to them that it is important to compromise because it's worth it to prevent the conflict. Encourage them to see the problem from the other person's perspective. It often makes it easier for people to compromise once they realize how the other person feels.

You cannot resolve a personality clash by acting as a go-between. You must bring together the two children involved to discuss the problem. It is their problem, and they must learn to resolve their own problems and not rely on you to sort them out. In any case, if you deal with the children separately, they will each wonder what was said about the problem when they weren't there.

Most personality-based conflicts between brothers and sisters revolve around the same few characteristics. For example, there are frequent blow-ups because one of your children is always slow and late for everything, while the other does things in a rush and hates hanging around waiting. Resolving this one, single problem could remove a sizeable proportion of the conflicts. Get to the root cause and deal with that, rather than tackle each incident individually.

The time to arrange this session is not when the children are busy bawling each other out, but later on when they are getting on fine and in a cooperative mood. You need to mediate, but get them to use these feedback techniques:

▸ Allow each to have a say without interruption from the other;
▸ Help them focus on the problem, not on personalities ("I get frustrated hanging around," not "You're always late for everything");

▸ Guide them to talk about their own feelings, not the other one's actions ("I feel stressed when you try to rush me").

Before you start the session, get them both to recognize that life would be more pleasant for everyone if this conflict were resolved. Then explain that this can only happen if they are both prepared to make some concessions. Make it clear that if they can't be reasonable and can't agree to a compromise, you will impose one, but you would rather they sorted it out.

Your role is to keep out of the discussion, except to remind them of the feedback techniques if they start to stray from them. Also, since you are only a referee, you must not express any personal view. You might personally agree that Jack is unreasonably slow at getting ready for anything, but it won't help if you say so. And even if he is, Ned has still got to learn to cope with it without losing his temper. Make sure that both of them are making a compromise, rather than one making all the concessions to keep things agreeable or because of a fear of reprisal.

Keep them at the discussion until they have agreed to a solution. Maybe Jack should be allowed to set the departure time (within reason), on condition that he then sticks to it. Ned may not get to leave as quickly as he'd like, but he can simply delay getting ready until two minutes before Jack's stipulated time. You may be able to help, too, by agreeing to give plenty of notice when you all need to go out as a family. Make no sudden announcements of "We're off shopping. Everyone ready?"

Once they've made their agreement, let them know that if the conflict continues, you'll have to sit them down again to find a better solution, or impose one of yours.

Finally, when they have made a decision, don't forget to comment on how effectively they addressed the problem (don't let on that half the adults you've met at work couldn't have done it).

One of the great things about employing team-building skills with your children is that the rewards keep growing. The more they feel like part of a team, the more they will want to cooperate with each other, and the fewer arguments they will have. You're doing them a big favor in helping them to strengthen their relationships. You're also doing yourself a big favor in making family life more enjoyable.

Conclusion

Once you realize how many skills you have already learned at work that you can apply at home, you'll find that it becomes natural to use them with your children. To begin with, you may wonder which skills to use when, but if you think about it, this isn't a worry at work. There, you barely think about most of these skills at all: they're instinctive. You don't remind yourself to smile every time a customer appears. You're probably barely even aware that you're doing it.

Building up the same portfolio of skills at home is a very similar process. You'll have found, reading this book, that some of the points really ring true, while others don't seem to apply to you at the moment. If you have only one child, for example, the team building skills won't have relevance to you.

So, practice the skills that are important to you at the moment. If you have a child who complains about the slightest thing ("I asked for my cocoa slightly hot, and you've given it to me very warm!"), master the tips for dealing with complaints. With a child like this, it won't be long before these skills become second nature.

If you have a second child, you'll find that after a couple of years you'll want to learn about team building in the family, maybe around the time your older child starts yelling, "I don't want a little brother, I hate him, and I wish he'd never been born!" You'll soon learn to incorporate team building tips into your repertoire and you'll practice them so instinctively that you won't even know you're doing it.

When your daughter hits the really mischievous stage, you'll learn about how to use discipline skills. When it gets really tough to elicit any kind of agreement from your teenager, you'll master negotiating skills (actually, you're doing well if you can get as far as the teenage years before you have to learn these). When your toddler interrupts constantly and then throws a tantrum if you don't respond instantly, you'll want to reread the section on customer relations tips and incorporate them into your parenting style.

Each time you encounter a behavioral problem that shows signs of becoming a habit, that's when you need to raid your business skills for another tip or two to add to your tool kit. Within a few years, you'll find that you're as skilled at parenting as you are in business. I'm afraid you won't get a promotion for your pains. But you will get an easier life, more fun, and at the end of the process, you'll have produced a terrific adult or two whose company you'll really enjoy. And if you play your cards right, they'll have all the skills they need to leave home successfully and give you some peace at last.

Index

Acknowledgment, 6, 9
Allowance, 34, 54, 59, 67-68
Arguments, 43
Alternatives, 29
Apologizing, 21-22

Behavior, modeling, 10, 16-18, 121
Benefits, 33
Boredom, 101
Bribery, 66
Buck, passing the, 103

Cartoons, 8, 14, 22, 32, 38, 46, 50, 56, 64, 70, 74, 84, 92, 100, 108, 114, 122
Children, self-centered, 33; strengths, 116-117; supporting each other, 107, 109-110
Choices, 39-40
Chores, 62, 63
Closing the sale, 36-41; alternative, 39-40; assumptive, 37-38; puppy dog, 41; question, 40
Communication, 65, 117-124
Compensating factors, 36
Complaints, 18-25, 125
Compromising, Confidentiality, 97
Conflict, 119-121, 123-124
Consistency, 6, 41, 98, 103
Control, 31, 41, 61
Cooperation, 7, 27
Criticism, 90-91, 96
Customer relations, 7-25, 125

Daydreaming, 101
Discipline, 81, 91-106, 125
Disney Corporation, 7
Division, 115

Enemy, parent as, 109

Family meals, 118
Features, 33
Feedback, 82-90; compromise, 90; feelings, 86-87; listening, 87-88; mistakes, 91; planning, 82-85; positive, 88; private, 85-86; solutions, 88-89
Friction, avoiding, 113

Homework, 61
Honesty, 55

Incentives, 66-76; 89; challenge, 73-75; freedom, 75-76; job satisfaction, 73; money, 67-68; recognition, 71, 76-79, 112-113; responsibility, 72; security, 68; status, 69
Interviews, 95-98

Judgements, avoiding, 83

Labels, 83-85, 88-89
Leeches, explanation of, 6
Listening, 19-20, 87-88; children who don't, 99-101

Management, 81-106
Managers, 61
Manipulators, 55, 102
McDonald's, 7
Mistakes, 90-91
Money, 67-68, 93-94, 97, 113
Motivation, 61-79; big picture, 62; communication, 65-66; incentives, 66-76; realistic targets, 63-65

Needs behind requests, 13-16
Negotiating, 43-60, 125; agreement, 58-60; aim high, 49-52; bottom line, 47-49; cards on the table, 54-56; concessions, 57-58; variables, 54-56; win-win deal, 44-47
Neutrality, 21

Objections, handling, 34-36; putting in context, 35
Objectives, setting, 28-29

Performance, 63, 93
Personality clash, 123
Prima donna behavior, 105-106
Problems, resolution of, 13-15, 24-25, 91-106
Punishment, 98, 102

Questions, asking, 23; open-ended, 15-16, 30-31

Respect, 17-18
Responsibility, 111-112
Rivalry, 119-124
Rules, 105

Security, 68
Selling, 27-41
Skills, practicing, 125; using, 5
Smiles, power of, 10-11, 125
Solutions, 24-25
Standards, 93-94
Status, 69
Strengths, 116-117
Sulking, 104-105
Support, 109-110
Sympathizing, 20

Tale-telling (tattling), 115-116
Targets, 63
Teamwork, 107-124, 125
Training, 112

Viewpoint, child's, 11-13, 33, 45

Whining, 5, 104